« LES ÉCHANGES »

(D'après le frontispice de l'*Histoire de l'Amérique septentrionale*,
de Bacqueville et Potherie).

The Map of New Scotland from Sir William Alexander's
'An Encouragement to Colonies' London, 1624

# TRANSATLANTIC VOYAGES
## 1600–1699
## Second Edition

## By David Dobson

CLEARFIELD

First Edition, 2004

Second Edition printed for
Clearfield Company by
Genealogical Publishing Co.
Baltimore, Maryland
2008

ISBN-13: 978-0-8063-5369-2
ISBN-10: 0-8063-5369-4

*Made in the United States of America*

# INTRODUCTION

## *Transatlantic Voyages, 1600–1699*
### Second Edition

During the seventeenth century, the smaller nations of northwestern Europe began to follow the example of England and France by establishing shipping links with North America and the West Indies. While the voyages made from English ports are well recorded, especially in the works of Peter Wilson Coldham, those from the other nations of northwestern Europe lie fragmented and scattered throughout archives and libraries on both sides of the Atlantic.

In 2004 I attempted to bring together evidence of voyages from Scandinavia, Germany, the Netherlands, France, Scotland, Ireland, Wales and the Channel Islands based on both primary and secondary sources in Europe and America. The interest in this topic stimulated further research, and over the last few years a considerable number of other voyages have been identified. These new discoveries have been incorporated along with the original data in a restructured form in a second edition. As records of voyages from Europe are far from complete for the period, evidence of vessels returning to Europe from the Americas has also been included. Exploratory voyages generally led to trade and subsequent settlement in the Americas. The vessels listed are therefore among those used by the original European settlers of colonial America. The ports of departure in Europe may well indicate the localities from where the first emigrants originated and therefore centers where genealogical research may be concentrated.

The vessels are listed alphabetically by name and chronologically by date of voyage for those with similar names.

David Dobson
St. Andrews, Scotland, 2008

## CARTE DE LA LOUISIANE

En l'Amérique Septentrionale, depuis la Nouvelle France jusqu'au Golfe de Mexique, en tout depuis le Pays que les Sauvages à découvert dans un grand continent depuis que ce dit de l'invention du Père Louis depuis a 23. les années 1679. 80. & 81.

GOLFE DE HUDSON

DETROIT DE HUDSON

NOUVELLE FRANCE

LA

LOUISIANE

NOUVELLE MEXIQUE

ISLES LUCAYES

NOVA SCOTIA

The Gulfe of: the Riuer of: Canada

West

South

North

East

Il. Brion

Il. Rama

Il. S.t Paul

PART OF NOVA FRANCIA

THE GRAND BAYE

Chateane

J. Michton

S.t Peter

Banc Aruidrie

Prima Insula Carolo Magno Britanniae Monarchae
Secus mouam Regwam, euns fundamenta
Camber.
Primus in Anglia R. Ethelfrythium

J. Deizes

S.t Thom. more

C. Gro

Insula olim vocata Noua Terra.
The Iland called of olde:

NEWFOVND LAND

Ascribed by Captaine John Mason, an industrious Gent:
who spent seuen years in the Country

Lacus incognitus
great Lake or Sea whowne
discouered in Anno 1615 by Captaine Mason

A Scale to English Leagues
5    10    15    20    25    30    35    40

Il. of Diamonds

C. Race    Trepassa    C.de paus
Glamorgans
Vauglaus
Bristoll
Romaia
Formosa
Farrelland    Carbonier
Bristoll
Trinita    Placentia    Placentia harbor
Fretum    harbor
C.de Spere

S.t Mary

S.t Ann's

S.t Brandons
Fayre
Forty

B.t Iames
B.t Charles
S.t Iames

S.t Francis bay

Trinitie bay

NORTH FALKLAND

Bay of Cupers

Bona Vista or Cabot prima terra
Reperta

Bay of Fogg

C.S.Iohn

Bel Nowlan

Port Noeulan

Port Granfranche

Gog

Bel Iile

B.s Aw

C.de groiss

Bellile

Paguin Ins:

Insula olim reperitur. Noua Terra a Cabatis Veneto primo
reperta, Anno Dni 1497, sub auspicijs & sumptibus Henrici
7.i Anglorum Regis super literas patentes a Rege data:
Et traditicia concessa 1577 Dna Humfredo Gilbert
Et quibi Anuotis Anno 1615 a Iacobo Regio Britanniae
Monarcha Societatis Nobilis generosis et Mercatorum
Londinensis et Bristoliensis concessa sub Magno Sigilo
Angliae. Cuius pars Australis de Cambriae portugals alter
ceteris Fretum Adentis Angliae, Insula Cambriole, alter
Guhdelma Vaughano Generossissimo vido cura et labore Io:
Annis Slany Societatis Tesoraruj Bermuda & Regularis
hanc nauim Henricum de suffulk Vaughanus Iecus maritima
cepit 157 Et postea, pertinens, insula Terrae Superranidd
perry, Richi Fleming ipse ad Capitali Petrie Vivide Plantavit
Dss georgio Caluert Baronis Ac: Baltimore Signaunti

VUE DE QUÉBEC AU DIX-SEPTIÈME SIÈCLE
(D'après J.-B.-L. Franquelin).

LEITH HARBOUR, 1680,
showing the King's Wark on the extreme right. Old Ship Inn, New Ship
Inn, and Mylne's Land, but no Signal Tower (built 1685).

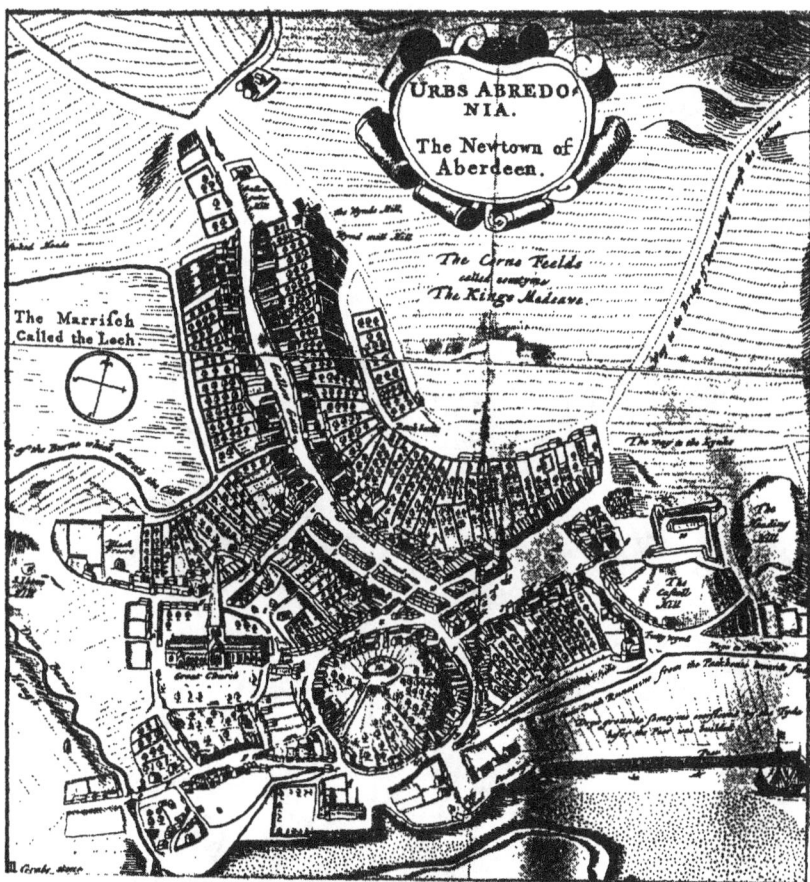

URBS ABREDO NIA.

The Newtown of Aberdeen.

The Gynde Hill
Bread mill Hill

The Corns Feelds
called commonie
The Kings Meidave

The Marrisch
Called the Loch

The way to the Gyde

The Spitell Hill

The Castell Hill

# SOURCES

## Archives

| | | |
|---|---|---|
| AA | = | Ayr Archives, Scotland |
| ARA | = | Algemeen Rijksarchief, The Hague |
| AZ | = | Archief van der Staten van Zeeland |
| BA | = | Barbados Archives |
| BL | = | British Library, London |
| BM | = | British Museum, London |
| BN | = | Bibliotheque Nationale, Paris |
| CLRO | = | Corporation of London Record Office |
| ECA | = | Edinburgh City Archives, Scotland |
| EUL | = | Edinburgh University Archives, Scotland |
| FCA | = | French Colonial Archives |
| FFA | = | French Ministry of Foreign Affairs Archives, Paris |
| GA | = | Glasgow Archives, Scotland |
| GAA | = | Gemeentarchief Amsterdam, Notoral Records |
| GAR | = | Gemeentarchief Rotterdam, Notariele Records |
| LCC | = | London Commissary Court, England |
| MUN | = | Memorial University, Newfoundland |
| NA | = | National Archives, London |
| NAC | = | National Archives of Canada |
| NAS | = | National Archives of Scotland, Edinburgh |
| NJSA | = | New Jersey State Archives, Trenton |
| NLS | = | National Library of Scotland, Edinburgh |
| NMM | = | Netherlands Maritime Museum |
| NYPL | = | New York Public Library |
| NYSA | = | New York State Archives, Albany |
| RAK | = | Rigs Arkivet, Kobenhavn, West Indian Chancery |
| SRA | = | Sverige Riksarkiv, Stockholm |

## Publications

| | | |
|---|---|---|
| ASC | = | Acadia at the end of the Seventeenth Century, J. C. Webster, [St John, New Brunswick, 1934] |
| ActsPCCol | | Acts of the Privy Council, Colonial, series |
| ASC | = | Acadia at the end of the 17th century. J. C. Webster, [St John, N.B., 1934] |
| BD | = | Les rochelais dans la vallee du Saint Laurent, [1599-1618], R. Le Blant and M.Delafosse, |

|  |  |  |
|---|---|---|
| | | [Quebec, 1956] |
| BNF | = | The Beginnings of New France, 1524-1663, P. Claxton, [Toronto, 1973] |
| CalSPDom | | Calendar of State Papers, Domestic, series |
| CalSPIre | | Calendar of State Papers, Ireland, series |
| CEC | = | Exiles of the Covenant, W. H. Carslow, [Helensburgh, Scotland, 1908] |
| CJR | = | Correspondence of Jeremias van Rensselaer, 1651-1674, [Albany, 1932] |
| CMR | = | Correspondence of Maria van Rensselaer, 1669-1689, [Albany, 1935] |
| CRB | = | No Peace Beyond the Line, the English in the Caribbean, 1624 – 1690, [New York, 1972] |
| CSP | = | Calendar of State Papers, Colonial, [London, 1860] |
| CTB | = | Calendar of Treasury Books, series |
| DBQ | = | 'Explorers and Colonies: America, 1500-1625', D.B. Quinn, [London, 1990] |
| DCB | = | Dictionary of Canadian Biography, [Toronto, 1966] |
| DI | = | Documents Illustrative of the History of the Slave Trade to America, [Washington, DC, 1930] |
| DNY | = | Documents Illustrative of the Colonial History of New York |
| DWI | = | Danish West Indies under Company Rule, 1671-1754, [New York, 1917] |
| FH | = | French History, series |
| GMNJ | = | Genealogical Magazine of New Jersey, series |
| HAF | = | Histoire des Antilles Francaises, P. Butel, [Paris, 2002] |
| HCF | = | Histoire de Colonies Francaises, G. Hainotaux, [Paris, 1929] |
| HDC | = | History of Delaware County, Pennsylvania, H. G. Ashmead, [Philadelphia, 1884] |
| HEA | = | History of Huguenot Emigration to America, C. W. Baird, [Baltimore, 1966] |
| HH | = | Holland on the Hudson, O. A. Rink, [New York, 1986] |
| HMC | = | Historical Manuscript Commission, London |
| HS | = | Hakluyt Society publications |
| IJMH | = | International Journal of Maritime History, series |
| ISE | = | In Search of Empire, the French in the Americas, 1670-1730, [Cambridge, 2004] |

JHC  =  Journal of the House of Commons, series
JJD  =  Journal of Jasper Danckaerts, 1679-1680,
        [New York, 1913]
JSIS  =  Journal of Scotch-Irish Studies, series
LPA  =  Les Petites Antilles, J. P. Moreau,
        [Paris, 1992]
MHM=  Maryland Historical Magazine, series
NNC  =  Prehistory of the Nieuw Netherlands Company,
        S. Hart, [Amsterdam, 1959]
NWI  =  New World Immigrants, M. Tepper,
        [Baltimore, 1979]
NYGBR  New York Genealogical Biographical Record
NYCM=  New York Colonial Manuscripts
OC  =  The Oates Collection, [Ottawa, 1940]
OSN  =  Old Scots Navy, 1689-1710,
        [London, 1914]
PA  =  Pennsylvania Archives, series
PFM  =  Personnes et Familles a la Martinique au XVIIe
        Siecle, J. Petitjean-Roget, [Paris, 2000]
PGSP=  Pennsylvania German Society, Proceedings
PMHB=  Pennsylvania Magazine of History & Biography
PNJHS=  Proceedings of the New Jersey Historical Society
RAC  =  Riches from Atlantic Commerce, [Leiden, 2003]
RB  =  Les arrest du parlement de Rouen du 25 Juin et
        les premieres companies du Canada, Robert Le
        Blant in *Revue des societies savants de Haute
        Normandie,* iii, [1956]

RCRB=  Records of the Convention of Royal Burghs
RL  =  Royal Letters, ...1621-1638, D. Laing,
        [Edinburgh, 1867]
RNA  =  Records of Nieuw Amsterdam, B. Fernow,
        [New York, 1897]
RPCS=  Register of the Privy Council of Scotland
RVC  =  Records of the Virginia Company of London.
        [Washington, DC, 1930s]
SD  =  Svenska oden vid Delaware, 1638-1831,
        N. Jacobsson, [Stockholm, 1938]
SH  =  The Pre-History of the New Netherlands
        Company, Simon Hart, [Amsterdam, 1959]
SHS  =  Scottish History Society, publications
SI  =  Scandinavian Immigrants in New York,
        1630-1674, J. O. Evjen, [Baltimore, 1995]

SPAWI     Calendar of State Papers, America and the
West Indies, series

SSD =     Swedish Settlements on the Delaware, 1638-64
A. Johnson, [New York, 1911]

TA =     The Atlantic, Paul Butel, [London, 1999]

TBL =     The Bolton Letters, 1697-1714,
A. L. Simon, [London, 1928]

TD =     Le Commerce rochelais de la fin du XVe siecle
au debut du XVII, E. Trocme and M. Delafosse,
[Paris, 1952]

THDT=     Trinity House, Deptford Transactions,
1609-1635, [London]

UJA =     Ulster Journal of Archaeology, series

VAC =     Virginia Admiralty Court Records

VDV =     Voyages of David de Vries, C.M.Parr, [1969]

VH =     Nederlanders in Amerika, J. Van Hinke,
[Groningen, 1928]

VRB =     Van Rensselaer Bowier ms, [Albany, 1908]

VSC =     Voyages of Samuel de Champlain, 1604-1618,
[New York, 1907]

WFM =     William Freeman's Letterbook, 1678-1684,
[Institute of Jamaica ms]

WMQ=     William and Mary Quarterly Journal, series

WPB =     Welsh Port Books, J. Lewis, [London, 1927]

WPD =     William Penn and the Dutch Migration to
Pennsylvania, W. I. Hull, [Swarthmore, 1935]

WSC =     Works of Samuel de Champlain, H. Biggar,
[Toronto, 1922]

XJVa =     Executive Journals of Virginia, series

# TRANSATLANTIC VOYAGES, 1600-1699
## Second and expanded edition

**Ships from or to the Americas and Scandinavia, Germany, the Netherlands, France, Scotland, Ireland, Wales and the Channel Islands.**

**ABRAHAMS OFFERHANDE,** [Abraham's Offering], from Amsterdam, Holland, to the Nieuw Nederland in 1654.[NYPL]

**ADVENTURE OF HULL,** master Lancelot Anderson, from Kinsale, Ireland, to Maryland, and return in 1667, she returned with the Virginia fleet to Land's End but was chased by a Dutch man'o'war to Bristol, England. [Acts PCCol#722/727][Cal.SPDom#1676/491]

**ADVENTURE,** from Kinsale, Ireland, to Barbados and the Leeward Islands in November 1674. [Cal.SPDom#1674/417]

**ADVENTURE,** Captain Clayton, from Nantes, France, via Montserrat, Nevis, and Antigua, to Boston, New England, in 1679. [WFL]

**ADVENTURE OF COLERAINE,** returned from Virginia and Maryland to Belfast, Ireland, in 1682. [CTB.VII.1525]

**ADVICE,** arrived in Kinsale, Ireland, from Nevis in September 1667. [Cal.SPIre#1667/449]

**AFRICANEN,** Captain Chaloupin, from Brandenburg to St Thomas, Virgin Islands, in March 1692. [RAK]

**AGREEMENT OF YOUGHAL,** master Joseph Harris, from Youghal, Ireland, via Nevis in the West Indies, to New England in 1681, attacked and plundered at sea by the Spanish possibly on the Lion of Havanna. [SPAWI#1680/1621][ActsPCCol#1682/62]

**AKER,** from the Netherlands to the Nieuw Nederland in 1639 and in 1641. [GAA#1500/1526]

**ALEXANDER,** master William Ramsay, from Scotland to
Nova Scotia in September 1628, returned to Loch Ryan.
[NAS.AC2.117]

**ALEXANDER,** 300 tons, master William Watson, from Cork,
Ireland, to the York River, Virginia, in 1654.
[NA.HCA.Exams.Vol.71]

**ALEXANDER OF GLASGOW,** master David Ferguson,
from Ayr, Scotland, to Virginia on 26 July 1681.
[NAS.E72.3.6]

**ALEXANDER OF INVERNESS,** [alias **MARY OF
INVERNESS**], master William Geddes, arrived in the
Delaware River, Pennsylvania, in 1683.
[CTB.VIII.212/1009]

**ALEXANDER OF INVERKEITHING,** master Thomas
Thomson, from Leith, Scotland, to Carolina and return in
1684 and 1686. [NAS.AC7.8; GD172/1585]

**AMERICA,** master Joseph Wasey, from Rotterdam in the
Netherlands via London bound for Philadelphia,
Pennsylvania, arrived there *with 80 passengers* on 30
August 1683. [PGSPro/1899/100]

**AMERICA MERCHANT OF STOCKTON,** master John
Brown or Brewer, from Leith via Aberdeen, Scotland,
*with passengers* bound for East New Jersey on 26
August 1685. [NAS.E72.1.13; E72.15.32]

**AMITY,** from Ireland *with passengers* bound for Virginia in
1653. [NA.Inter-regnum Entry Book #98/405]

**AMITY OF BOSTON,** master Lott Gordon, arrived in Port
Glasgow, Scotland, on 31 August 1691 from New
England. [NAS.E72.15.21]

**ANN AND HESTER,** from Ireland *with passengers* bound for
Boston, New England, in April 1680.
[UJA#2/1/274][SPAWI.1682/441]

**ANN AND MARY OF KINSALE,** master George Somerset, arrived in Kinsale, Ireland, on 30 September 1669 from the Leeward Islands. [CSPIre]

**ANNE MARIE DE LA ROCHELLE.** [The Anne Mary of La Rochelle], master Samuel Thomas, from France to Quebec in 1698. [Gironde archives ms]

**ANTELOPE OF GLASGOW,** arrived in Dunbarton, Scotland, from Martinique in 1647. [GA: Dunbarton Register of Ship Entries, 1595-1658]

**ANTELOPE OF BELFAST,** master Edward Cooke, arrived in Philadelphia, Pennsylvania, on 9 October 1682 *with 7 passengers* from Ireland. [PMHB#8/9]

**ANTELOPE,** master Cabel Chapin, from Glasgow, Scotland, to Pennsylvania, the Chesapeake, and the West Indies, in 1693. [NAS.CS29/1752][GA:Shawfield mss#1.42-43]

**ARABELLA,** master John Lethun, from Cork, Ireland, *with passengers* bound for Barbados in 1689. [ActsPCCol.1689#274/10]

**AREN,** [The Eagle], from Sweden to Nya Sverige, (New Sweden), before 1656. [DNY#1/606]

**ARENT,** [The Eagle],master Pieter Claessen Deucht, arrived in Nieuw Amsterdam in July 1662; from Holland *with 11 passengers* bound for the Nieuw Nederland in 1664; from the Nieuw Nederland on 17 August 1664 bound for the Netherlands. [DNY#2/454][HH#166]

**ARMAN DE SOUDER,** master Jacques Doridan, from Chevelet on the River Bordeaux, France, to Newfoundland, captured by the Dutch on the return voyage in 1673 and taken to Plymouth, England. [ActsPCCol.1674/975]

**BACHELOR OF BRISTOL,** from Kinsale, Ireland, on 26 October 1669 bound for Nevis, [Cal. SPIreland.1669/18]; master Samuel Gibbons, *with passengers* probably from

Scotland, arrived in St Mary's County, Maryland, during November 1674. [MSA.Early Settlers Book#152]

**BACHELOR,** master Adrian van Dort, from New York via Cadiz, Spain, to Amsterdam, Holland, in 1673, but was captured and taken to Plymouth, England. [NA.HCA.Vol.77/5.1674]

**BACHELOR,** a ketch, from St Martin, Isle de Re, France, via Waterford, Ireland, to Nevis and Montserrat in 1678. [WCL][CRB#323]

**BACHELOR OF BOSTON,** a brigantine, master Thomas Eyre, from Port Glasgow, Scotland, to Madeira during September 1691. [NAS.E72.15.22]

**BADINE,** from Brest, France, on 24 October 1698 bound for Louisiana. [ASC#181]

**BARBADOS MERCHANT,** master Robert Williamson, from Barbados in 1665 bound for Berwick, England, landed in Leith, Scotland, on 7 July 1665, [ActsPCCol.1666/668]; arrived in Leith, Scotland, on 15 November 1665 from Barbados, [NAS.E72.15.2]; master Cuthbert Sharples, arrived in Port Glasgow, Scotland, in July 1689 from Virginia; arrived in Port Glasgow via Beaumaris, Wales, from Virginia on 12 February 1691. [NAS.E72.19.14/21; RD3.87.173]

**BARBARA OF COLERAINE,** from Beaumaris, Wales, to the Leeward Islands in 1695, [ActsPCCol.1695/577, 21], master John Baker, arrived in Port Glasgow, Scotland, on 23 May 1696 from Antigua. [NAS.E72.15.23]

**BELLE,** 60 tons, from La Rochelle, France, on 24 July 1684 *with passengers* bound for the Mississippi, arrived in Haiti in December 1684, from there bound for the Mississippi but wrecked on Matagordo Peninsula in 1686.[DCB.I.180]

**BELLE MADELON,** [The Lovely Madeleine], 60 tons, master Michel Achard, from La Rochelle, France, to

Acadia and to the West Indies in 1684. [Charente Maritime archives]

**BELLIQUEUX DE LA ROCHELLE,** [The Warlike of La Rochelle], 250 tons, master Jean De La Grange, from La Rochelle, France, via Canada to the West Indies in 1673 and in 1697. [B.N.Melanges de Colbert#165] [La Rochelle archives]

**BENEFIT OF KINSALE,** arrived in Kinsale, Ireland, in June 1669, probably from Virginia. [Cal.SPIreland.1669/159]

**BENJAMIN OF GLASGOW,** master Robert Greenfield, from Port Glasgow, Scotland, to the West Indies on 7 August 1681. [NAS.E72.19.4]

**BENJAMIN AND MARY,** master Richard Smith, arrived in Kilmare, Ireland, from Virginia, in November 1699. [CTB.XV.417]

**BETTY OF BRISTOL,** a sloop, from Youghal, Ireland, in May 1696, via Funchal, Madeira, bound for Antigua. [TBL#40]

**BETTY OF CORK,** an 80 ton galley, arrived in Virginia during 1700. [NA.CO5.1441]

**BETTY,** from Jamaica to Cork in 1705. [CalSPDom.SP63/365/127]

**BIEN AYMEE DE BAYONNE,** [The Very Friendly of Bayonne], from France to Newfoundland in 1696. [Charente Maritime archives, B235/345]

**BLESSING OF AYR,** a bark, from Ayr, Scotland, to Barbados and St Kitts and return in 1644. [NAS.B6.12.9]

**BLESSING OF KINSALE,** 40 tons, master Peter Jeffreys, with 12 men as crew, from Kinsale, Ireland, to Masterlin Bay, and Caplin Bay, Newfoundland, in 1676. [NA.CO1/38, 1676, 223/4]

**BLESSING OF BOSTON,** master Nathaniel Warden, from Port Glasgow, Scotland, to New England in November 1682. [NAS.E72.19.8]

**BLOSSOM,** from Leith, Scotland, *with passengers* to Barbados in August 1680. [NAS.HH.1.11][RPCS.VI.456]

**BONADVENTURE OF IRVINE,** returned to Ayr, Scotland, from Barbados and St Kitts in 1646, [see Robert Rowan/Rolland's testament, confirmed 23 November 1648 and 4 August 1649 with the Commissariat of Glasgow, NAS]; arrived in Ayr, Scotland, from the West Indies in 1647. [AA]

**BONAVENTURE,** [The Good Risk], from St Malo, France, to the Magdalen Islands, Canada, 1591, captured by a Bristol privateer on the return voyage. [DCB.1.409]

**BONAVENTURE,** [The Good Risk], when bound from Newfoundland to St Valery, France, was captured and taken to Weymouth, England, in 1639. [NA.HCA.13/55/324]

**BONAVENTURE DE DIEPPE,** [The Good Risk of Dieppe], master James de Senne, to Jamaica in 1658. [Cal.SPDom.XIII.218]

**BON COUER,** [The Good Heart], a privateer, from La Rochelle, France, bound for Quebec in 1697, but captured off Newfoundland and taken to London. [NA.HCA.Exams.Vol.81]

**BON DIEU,** [The Good God], master Emery de Caen, from France to Quebec in 1631. [SPAWI.1631/23]

**BON ESPOIR,** [The Good Spirit], from Honfleur, France, to Newfoundland in 1597; from Honfleur, France, in 1600 bound for Tadoussac. [DCB.I.209][BNF#64]

**BON FRANCOIS,** [The Good Francis], 90 tons, arrived in Quebec during August 1649. [NAC]

**BONNE RENOMEE,** from Honfleur, France, Captain Jean Girot, bound for Tadoussac on the St Lawrence River on 15 March 1603, arrived there on 26 May 1603. [BNF#74/76][DCB.I.188]

**BORDEAUX MERCHANT,** 145 tons, master Laurence Starman, from Kinsale, Ireland, to Jamaica in 1691. [ActsPCCol.1690#364/289]

**BOSTON MERCHANT,** master Marck Hunkens, from Port Glasgow, Scotland, to Virginia in October 1685. [NAS.E72.19.8]

**BOUFFONE,** [The Jester], from Canada to France in 1677. [B.N.Melanges de Colbert#175]

**BRETONNE DE LA ROCHELLE,** [The Brittany of La Rochelle], 90 tons, master Jean Borny, from La Rochelle, France, to Quebec in 1682/1683; master Simon Pierre Denys, from La Rochelle on 8 April 1694 *with passengers* bound for Acadia. [ASC#165][Charente Maritime archives, B235/129]

**BURG VON STADE** [The Town of Stade], master Sander sanders, arrived in the Wicomico River, St Mary's County, Maryland, from Bremen, [a Swedish possession in Germany] in 1671. [SRA:Stockholm.Angelica.VII.543]

**CALEDONIA,** from Leith Scotland, *with passengers* to Darien on the Isthmus of Panama on 14 July 1698, returned to Scotland via New York in 1699. [NAS.CC8.8.83]

**CARDINALE,** from Le Havre, France, *with passengers* to St Kitts on 16 February 1627, landed on 8 May 1627. [BN][TA#1118]

**CARDINALE,** 300 tons, arrived in Quebec during August 1645; master Pierre Le Gardeur de Repentigny, from France to Quebec in 1646; master Jean Poitiel, from France *with passengers* bound for Quebec and Montreal in 1648, arrived in Quebec on 20 August 1648; Captain

Jammes, arrived in Quebec on 8 September 1650.
[NAC][DCB.I.47]

**CAROLINA MERCHANT,** 170 tons, master James Gibson,
from Gourock, Scotland, *with 148 passengers* bound for
Port Royal, South Carolina, on 21 July 1684, arrived in
Charleston on 2 October 1684; from Glasgow, Scotland,
to the Caribee Islands on 29 April 1686. [NAS.AC7/8;
E72.19.12][RPCS.VII.710][NA.CO5.287.126]

**CAROLUS SECONDUS,** master Isaac Foxcroft, to Virginia
in 1675. [PCCol.1675/2]

**CASTEEL VAN SLUYS,** master Jan Jacobsen de Vosch,
arrived in Middelburg, Zealand, in 1643 from Virginia;
master Anthonis Luester, from Barbados to the
Netherlands in 1644. [GAR.86.294.559; 86.336.637]

**CASTLE OF STOCKHOLM,** a Swedish ship at Barbados in
1667.[PCCol.1668/743]

**CAT,** a yacht, from the Netherlands to Curacao in 1644.
[DNY.1/165]

**CATHERINE,** master Thomas Chefdostel, from Rouen,
France, *with passengers* to the Ile de Sable, Canada, in
1597, also *with passengers* in 1598, in 1599, 1600, 1601,
and 1603. [DCB.I.210/421]

**CATHERINE OF LONDON,** master Edward Thomson,
arrived in Dundee, Scotland, on 20 October 1637 from
the West Indies. [DA.dsl]

**CATHERINE DE LA ROCHELLE,** [Cathereine of La
Rochelle], 100 tons, master Thare Chaillaud, from La
Rochelle, France, to Quebec in 1666, and in 1667 under
master Jean Chaille. [La Rochelle Archives]

**CATHERINE OF GLASGOW,** master John Philp, from
Glasgow, Scotland, to Charlestown, New England, on 25
April 1673, [NAS.E72.16.4]; master John Leckie, from
Port Glasgow to New England in September 1682, also

in October 1685, also on 17 September 1684.
[NAS.E72.19.6/9]

**CATHERINE OF HOLLAND,** Captain Chaviteau, from
France to Quebec in 1691. [Charente Maritime Archives]

**CATHERINE OF LONDONDERRY,** arrived in Somerset
County, Maryland, in 1692. [SPAWI.1692/2295]

**CATHERINE DE LA ROCHELLE,** [The Catherine of La
Rochelle], 180 tons, master Jean Thomas, from La
Rochelle, France, to Canada and the West Indies in 1695.
[Charente Maritime Archives, B5691]

**CATHOLIQUE,** [The Universal], master Pierre Belain, from
Le Havre, France, *with passengers* to St Kitts and
Barbados on 24 February 1627, arrived in St Kitts on 8
May 1627. [HCF.I.392][TA#118]

**CHARDON,** 50 tons, master Michel Coste, from Le Havre,
France, on 19 January 1583 *with 30 passengers*, arrived
at Cape Breton on 7 February 1583.
[DCB.I.87][DBQ#288]

**CHARITAS,** master Jan Jochimsen, from Stockholm, Sweden,
via Gothenburg, Sweden, and La Rochelle, France,
bound for Nya Sverige, (New Sweden), *with passengers*
in 1641, and possibly in 1644.
[PMBH.III.462][SSD#759]

**CHARITAS,** master John Harloe, to Virginia in 1675.
[PCCol.1675/2]

**CHARITY,** 60 tons, master Edward Kenton, from New
England to Bilbao, Portugal, in 1667.
[SPAWI.1667/1459]

**CHARLES,** from St Malo, France, probably to Tadoussac,
Canada, 1591. [DCB.1.409]

**CHARLES OF BRISTOL,** arrived in Kinsale, Ireland, from
Barbados on 18 November 1667. [Cal.SPIre.1667/486]

**CHARLES OF LEITH,** from Leith, Scotland, *with passengers* to Virginia or Barbados in June 1669. [RPCS.III.21]

**CHARLES OF GUERNSEY,** master Nicholas Thoumes, from Newfoundland to Alicante, Spain, in 1675. [ActsPCCol.1676/1069]

**CHARLES OF LONDON,** 130 tons, from Amsterdam, Holland, bound for the West Indies, captured in August 1678 by the Spanish at Buenos Ayres on the River Plate. [ActsPCCol.1680/1342]

**CHARLES OF NEW YORK,** a flute ship, master Thomas Singelton, from Amsterdam, Holland, *with passengers* bound for New York on 26 June 1679, arrived on 23 September 1679, returned to Holland from Boston, New England, on 23 July 1680 via the Orkney Islands and London. [JJD]

**CHARLES OF GLASGOW,** master John Murray, from Port Glasgow, Scotland, to Carolina in June 1684. [NAS.E72.19.9]

**CHARLES OF BELFAST,** master Robert Arthur, arrived in Port Glasgow, Scotland, on 1 September 1691 from Montserrat. [NAS.E72.15.21]

**CHARLES OF GLASGOW,** master Robert Arthur, arrived in Port Glasgow, Scotland, on 20 March 1691 from the West Indies, from Port Glasgow to the West Indies in April 1691. [NAS.E72.15.22]

**CHARLOTTE AMELIA,** master Daniel Moy, at St Thomas in the Virgin Islands in February 1686. [DWI]

**CHARLOTTE LOVISE,** from Brandenburg to St Thomas, Virgin Islands, in June 1693. [RAK]

**CHAT BOUQUE,** captured at sea by the English when bound for Quebec in 1655. [NAC]

**CHATEAUFORT,** [The Strong Castle], from France to Port
Royal, Acadia, in 1654. [NAC]

**CHRISTIANUS QUINTUS,** [Christian V], from Denmark to
St Thomas in the Virgin Islands, in September 1687;
master Jorgen Grabenen, from Denmark to Guinea and
St Thomas in the Virgin Islands in August 1698; from
Denmark via Guinea to St Thomas in the Virgin Islands.
[RAK][DWI]

**CHURCH OF BRISTOL,** Captain Popplestone, arrived in
Kinsale, Ireland, from Barbados on 22 September 1668.
[Cal.SPIre.1668/645]

**CHUR PRINCESSINDEN,** master Jacob Lambert, from
Brandenburg to St Thomas, Virgin Islands, in August
1690; Captain Wegman, from Brandenburg to St
Thomas, Virgin Islands, in June 1693;
master Peter Van Becke, from Brandenburg to St
Thomas, Virgin Islands, in March 1698. [RAK]

**CHUR PRINZ,** to St Thomas, Virgin Islands, in 1690; master
Wouter Ypes, from Emden, Germany, via Guinea to St
Thomas in November 1696. [DWI]

**CLEMENT,** [The Mild], from La Rochelle, France, via
Boston, New England, on 14 July 1663 bound for Port
Royal, Acadia. [NAC]

**CLERBAULT,** 80 tons, master Jacques Hurtain, from La
Rochelle, France, to Acadia and Quebec in 1667. [La
Rochelle Archives]

**COLOMBE,** [The Dove], master Mallet de Noisell, from
Bordeaux, France, to Canada in 1689. [Gironde
Archives, #6b1093]

**COLOMBE DE LA ROCHELLE,** [The Dove of La
Rochelle], 60 tons, master Jean Requiem, from La
Rochelle, France, to Quebec in 1696. [La Rochelle
Archives]

**COLOMBE MOUILLEE,** [The Tethered Dove], arrived in
Quebec in 1654; arrived in Quebec in 1655. [NAC]

**COMPANION,** master John Thomson, from Gravesend,
England, via Ireland to Barbados and New England in
June 1663. [NA.HCA.Exams#75]

**COMTE DE FRONTENAC DE LA ROCHELLE,**[The
Count of Frontenac of La Rochelle], 150 tons, master
Jean Couillandeau, from Bordeaux, France, to Quebec in
1699. [Gironde Archives #6b298]

**CONCLUSION,** probably from Scotland to Barbados in 1679.
[RPCS.VII.152]

**CONCORD,** master William Jeffries, from Rotterdam,
Zealand, *with passengers* bound for Philadelphia,
Pennsylvania, on 24 July 1683. [WPD#337]

**CONCORD,** from Marseilles, France, in September 1687 *with
90 Huguenot passengers* bound for St Domingo, arrived
there in February 1688. [HEA#224]

**CONCORDANCE,** from Leith, Scotland, via Aberdeen,
Scotland, *with passengers* bound for Virginia in August
1668. [Aberdeen City Archives: Aberdeen Town Council
letters]

**CONINGEN DAVID VON HAMBURG,** [King David of
Hamburg], trading with Virginia or Barbados in 1674.
[PCCol.1674/1006]

**CONINGS VAPEN,** [The King's Arms], master Jacob
Mailard, from Brandenburg to St Thomas, Virgin
Islands, in September 1692. [RAK]

**CONPUIS DE LA ROCHELLE,** 160 tons, master Matieu
Martin, from France to Quebec in 1696. [Charente
Maritime archives B5292]

**CONSENT OF BRISTOL or POOLE,** 130 tons, master
William Cock, via Ireland to the West Indies in 1691.
[ActsPCCol.1691#364/57]

**CONSTANTINOPLE,** Captain Ward, arrived in Kinsale, Ireland, from the West Indies in June 1667. [Cal.SPIre.1667#390]

**CONTENT,** master Tibault Suxbridge, from Baltimore, Ireland, via the West Indies to Newfoundland in 1609. [NA.HCA.13/226]

**COSTLY OF LONDON,** master Thomas Hamond, from Nevis to Limerick in 1631. [NA.HCA.13/50/367]

**COUR VOLANT,** Captain La Vivon, at Port Royal, Jamaica, 1673. [SPAWI.1673.21]

**COUVERTINE,** in Jamaica before 1658, [see Thomas Abbott's probate 1658 PCC, NA]; master John Lightfoot, from London via Leith, Scotland, *with passengers* to Virginia in September 1668. [RPCS.II.503/534][NA.HCA.Exams#77/11.1671]

**CROWN OF LONDON,** master Thomas Teddico, from Leith, Scotland, *with passengers* bound for the American Plantations in November 1679, shipwrecked off the Orkney Islands in December 1679. [CEC#212/5]

**DAME ANNE DE LA ROCHELLE,** [The Lady Anne of La Rochelle], 250 tons, master Helies Raymond, from France, arrived in Quebec on 19 September 1675. [Quebec Archives]

**DANIEL OF DUBLIN,** in Maryland, 1666. [Accomack County Order Book]

**DANIEL VAN AMSTERDAM,** [The Daniel of Amsterdam], a pink, was condemned by the Governor of Maryland in May 1699. [SPAWI.1699/433]

**DAS WAPPEN DE HERZOGIN VON KURLAND,** [The Arms of the Duke of Courland], master Willem Mollens, from Courland bound for New Courland (alias Tobago), arrived there on 20 May 1654.

**DAUPHIN,** [The Dolphin], 200 tons, Captain Baudoin, arrived in Quebec in June 1644. [NAC]

**DAUPHIN DE LA ROCHELLE,** [The Dolphin of La Rochelle], 180 tons, master Jean Faure, from Bordeaux, France, to Newfoundland, Canada, and the West Indies in 1695. [Charente Maritime Archives B5691]

**DAVID VAN DORDRECHT,** [David of Dordrecht], a yacht, from Brazil and the West Indies to the Netherlands in 1624. [GAR.ONA.161.25.31]

**DAVID VON LUBECK,** [David of Lubeck], master John Ire, from Havanna, Cuba, in June 1630 bound for Germany, arrived in Plymouth, England, on 22 July 1630. [SPAWI.1630/100]

**DE ARENDT,** [The Eagle], master Pieter Claessen Deucht, arrived in Nieuw Amsterdam on 13 July 1662 from the Netherlands, and returned there in July 1662; master Pieter Corneliszon Bes, from the Netherlands *with 13 passengers* in March 1663 bound for the Nieuw Nederland; from Holland in 1664 *with 11 passengers* bound for the Nieuw Nederland, from there on 17 August 1664 bound for the Netherlands. [CJR#293] [NYCol.Mss#14/83-123][DNY#2/4544, 466][HH#166]

**DE ARENDT ZWART,** [The Black Eagle], Admiral Lucifer, from the Netherlands *with passengers* bound for the Amazon in 1624-1625. [HS.2$^{nd}$ series. 171.80]

**DE ARMUYDEN,** from Zealand *with passengers* to Guiana in 1628. [HS.2$^{nd}$ series, 56/133]

**DE BEER,** [The Bear], from Amsterdam, Holland, to the South River, the Nieuw Nederland, *with 33 passengers* in 1657. [PA.2.7/498]

**DE BERCH,** from Brazil to the Netherlands in 1654. [GAR.ONA.146.97.393]

**DE BEURS VAN COPENHAGEN,** [The Exchange of Copenhagen], {later renamed the Fridericus Quartus},

from St Thomas in the Danish West Indies to
Copenhagen, Denmark, arrived there on 28 April 1699.
[Sound Toll Registers]

**DE BEVER,** [The Beaver], from the Netherlands *with
passengers* bound for the Nieuw Nederland in 1656;
from Amsterdam, Holland, to the South River, the Nieuw
Netherlands, *with 11 passengers* in 1657; master Jan
Reyersen van der Beets, from the Netherlands on 25
April 1659 bound for the Nieuw Nederland; from there
to the Netherlands in September 1659; master Pieter
Reyersen van der Beets, to the Nieuw Nederland *with 51
passengers* in May 1661; master Pieter Reyersen van de
Beets, *with passengers* to the Nieuw Nederland in
January 1664, arrived there on 30 April 1664; Captain
Jacob, arrived in New York *with passengers* in 1679;
from Dextel Bay to Holland on 14 March 1680; from
New York on 17 November 1681 to the Netherlands;
from the Netherlands via Bermuda to New York in
August 1682; from New York to Amsterdam in July
1683; arrived in New York by September 1684 from
Amsterdam [CJR#147/171][CMR#55/80/112/163]
[PA.2.7/498][NYCol.MSS#14/83-123][DNY#2/452,
468][HH#166][JJD]

**DE BLAUWE DUIF,** [The Blue Dove], master Jan Jansen
Bestevaer, from Texel, Holland, bound for the Nieuw
Nederland in 1656. [NMM]

**DE BLAUWEN HAEN,** [The Blue Hen], master Cornelis
Oldemarckt, from Amsterdam, Holland, bound for the
Nieuw Nederland in 1644. [NMM]

**DE BLOESEM,** [The Blossom], from New York to the
Netherlands in October 1678. [CMR.26]

**DE BLYDE BOOTSCHAP,** [The Happy Message], master
Cornelis Jacobsen Mey, from Hoorn, Holland, to the
Nieuw Nederland in November 1620. [DNY#1/24]

**DE BONTE KOE,** [The Spotted Cow], from the Netherlands
*with passengers* bound for the Nieuw Nederland in
1656; from the Nieuw Nederland in August 1656 bound

for Holland; master Pieter Lucaszoon, *with 23
passengers* bound for the Nieuw Nederland on 15 April
1660; from the Nieuw Nederland in September 1660
bound for the Netherlands; master Jan Berge, from the
Netherlands to the Nieuw Nederland *with 93 passengers*
in April 1663, and returned in September 1663; from
Nieuw Amsterdam on 29 September 1665 *with 86
passengers* bound for the Netherlands.
[DNY#2/466][HH#166]
[CJR#30/236/242/329][NYCol.MSS#13/88, 14/83-123]

**DE BRANDARIS,** from Amsterdam, Holland, in September
1641 bound for the Nieuw Nederland. [NMM]

**DE BRANDENBURG,** master Jan Cornelissen Kuyper, from
Fort Kyck, Overal, Rio Essequibo, to Middelburg,
Zealand, in August 1700. [SPAWI.1700/715]

**DE BRANT VAN TROYEN,** [The Fire of Troy], arrived in
the Nieuw Nederland in January 1638 from the
Netherlands; from Amsterdam, Holland, *with passengers*
to the Nieuw Nederland in 1639. [VDV] [NYHM#1/196;
#1/215][GAA.inv#155a/583]

**DE BRUYNVISCH,** [The Brown Fish], master Jacob Claesen
Bruynnincx, from Delftshaven, the Netherlands, to Brazil
in 1642; a Dutch prize taken at Barbados in 1655; master
Cornelis Maertsen, from Amsterdam, Holland, to Nieuw
Amsterdam in the Nieuw Nederland *with 33 passengers*
in 1658; from the Netherlands on 19 June 1659 bound
for the Nieuw Nederland. [GAR.ONA.86.262.489]
[NYCol.mss#14/86/10][SI][SPAWI.1655/1979]

**DE CATTE,** from Middelburg, Zealand, to Guyana in 1600.
[ARA.SG.RGP#85/343]

**DE COOPMAN,** [The Merchant], from Amsterdam, Holland,
to New Orange in the Nieuw Nederland, and return in
1674; master Minne Jansz, from Amsterdam in
December 1673 via Curacao to Nieuw Amsterdam (New
York),arriving by July 1674, and from there to
Amsterdam. [NMM][CJR#460]

**DE CRAEN,** master Jan Corneliszoon May, from Amsterdam, Holland, to New France in 1611-1612.

**DE DOLFIJN VAN MIDDELBURG,** [The Dolphin of Middelburgh], was captured and taken to Barbados in 1701. [SPAWI.1702/1012]

**DE DOLPHIJN,** [The Dolphin], master Jacob Teunesen, from Texel, Holland, bound for Nieuw Amsterdam in September 1637. [NMM]

**DE DRAETVAT,** [The Wire-Cask], master Jan Jansen Besteveer, from the Netherlands *with passengers* bound for the Nieuw Nederland in 1657; from Amsterdam to the Nieuw Nederland in January 1658. [NYCol.ms#14/83-123][NWI.I.124][CJR#84]

**DE DRIE CONINGEN,** [The Three Kings], master Balthasar Willemszoon, from Madeira to the Netherlands in 1609; from Amsterdam, Holland, bound for the Nieuw Nederland in 1628. [GAR.ONA.14.120.392][NMM]

**DE DUIF,** [The Pigeon], from Amsterdam, the Netherlands, *with Walloon passengers* to the Amazon, arrived there in October 1623. [HS.2$^{nd}$ series, 56/lxxx; 2$^{nd}$ series, 171/258][BL.Sloane ms#179B]

**DE EENDRACHT VAN HOORN,** [The Concord of Hoorn], master Jacques le Maire, from the Netherlands on 15 July 1615 via south of the Magellan Strait bound for the East Indies, arrived in Jakarta on 20 September 1616. [HS.2$^{nd}$ series, XVIII]

**DE EENDRACHT,** [The Concord], master Adrien Joriszoon Thienpont, from Amsterdam, Holland, *with passengers* to Nieuw Amsterdam in January 1624, and returned to Amsterdam in June 1624; master Jan Cornelissen Speulman, from the Texel, the Netherlands, to Brazil, 1624; from Texel, Holland, *with 15 passengers* bound for Nieuw Amsterdam on 21 March 1630, arrived there on 24 May 1630; from Amsterdam *with 11 passengers* bound for Renselaerwijk, Nieuw Nederland, in July 1631; from the Nieuw Netherlands via Plymouth,

England, to the Netherlands in 1632; from Texel *with 12 passengers* bound for Nieuw Amsterdam in May 1634; from Texel on 8 October 1636 *with passengers*, arrived in Nieuw Amsterdam on 4 March 1637; to the Nieuw Nederland in 1643; master Willem Jopper, from Virginia to the Netherlands in 1650; at St Kitts and Montserrat in 1654-1655; master Jan Bergen, to the Nieuw Nederland *with 38 passengers* in April 1664, arrived there on 19 July 1664; from the Nieuw Nederland to the Netherlands in December 1664; from Holland to Bridegetown, Barbados, in 1668; master Joris Adriansen, from Essequibo and Berbice to Middleburg, Zealand, in 1700. [GAR.ONA.78.201.406] [DNY#1/46, 432, 468] [SI] [SPAWI.1632/62; 1667/1774; 1700/715] [GAA#917] [Cal.SPCol.VI/154][CJR#362] [GAR.ONA.135.324.437/1239.51.109]

**DE EENHEID,** [The Unity], Captain Regenwyn, at Ferryland, Newfoundland, 1673. [NA.CO1.34.37/85]

**DE EENHORN VAN ENKHUIZEN,** [The Unicorn of Enkhuizen], from the Netherlands to Newfoundland in the mid-1620s. [GAA.NA]

**DE EENHOORN VAN VLISSINGEN,** [The Unicorn of Flushing], from Kinsale, Ireland, to the Leeward Islands on 24 December 1667. [Cal.SPIre.1667/532]

**DE FAEM,** to Curacoa in 1655; from New York to Amsterdam, Holland, in June 1670; master Jacob Mouritszoon, from New York to Amsterdam in September 1671; from Amsterdam to New York in 1672. [GAR.ONA.231.135.239] [CJR#431/446][NMM]

**DEFIANCE,** 75 tons, master David Cousins, with a 10 man crew, from Youghal, Ireland, to St John's, Newfoundland, in 1677. [NA.CO1/41{1677} 168/170]

**DE FORT VAN ALBANY VAN NIEUW YORCK,** [The Fort of Albany of New York], from Amsterdam, Holland, to New York in 1669. [PCCol.1669/842]

**DE FORTUYN VAN HOORN,** [The Fortune of Hoorn], master Cornelius Jacobszoon Mey, arrived at Cape Mey, Delaware Bay, in 1614.

**DE FORTUYN,** [The Fortune] master Henrick Corstiaenssen, from the Netherlands to the Nieuw Nederland before 1615. [DNY#1/11]

**DE FORTUYN,** [The Fortune], master Abraham Pieters, from Madeira to Holland in 1631; master Aelbert Jocchems, from Rotterdam to Pernambuco and St Maertens in 1633; master Reyer Pietersz., from Barbados to the Netherlands in 1645.
[GAR.ONA.141.273.422/144.251.504/153.323.459]

**DE FORTUYN VAN AMSTERDAM,** [The Fortune of Amsterdam], master Cornelius Renard Uppranchard, at Jamaica in 1668. [SPAWI.1668.1707]

**DE FORTUYN,** from the Netherlands to Essequibo, arrived on 10 April 1702, and returnèd to Holland.
[SPAWI.1702/699]

**DE FRANCISCUS,** [The Francis], from Virginia to Delfthaven, the Netherlands, in 1643.
[GAR.ONA.204.288.435]

**DE FRIEDENBURG,** master Jacon Powellson, arrived *with passengers* in Nya Sverige (New Sweden) around 1640.
[Winthrop.II.76]

**DE GEKRUYSTE HART,** [The Broken Heart], master Dirck Jabobssen de Vries, from Amsterdam, Holland, in January 1664 *with 8 passengers* bound for the Nieuw Nederland, arrived in Nieuw Amsterdam on 21 April 1664, also arrived there on 1 August 16645 and returned to the Netherlands by 16 September 1664; master Siewart Dircksen, from Amsterdam in November 1664 bound for the Nieuw Nederland. [DNY#2/438, 468, 504] [HH#166]

**DE GELDERSE BLOM,** [The Flower of the Gelderland], master Cornelis Coenraetszoon van Kampen, from

Amsterdam, Holland, *with 12 passengers* to the Nieuw
Nederland in 1651; annual transatlantic voyages 1651 to
1657; from Amsterdam, Holland, to the Nieuw
Nederland on 4 August 1654; master Symen Clasen,
from Amsterdam *with 11 passengers* to the South River,
Nieuw Nederland in 1657, arrived there in April 1657;
from Nieuw Amsterdam to Amsterdam in May 1657.
[GAA#1096][CJR#11/14/38/42/47][DNY#2/5] [PA#2/7,
498][NYCol.ms.14/83-123]

**DE GOEDE HOOP,** [The Good Hope], from Amsterdam,
Holland, to the Nieuw Nederland in 1632. [NMM]

**DE GRATIE,** [The Mercy], from New York to Amsterdam,
Holland, in March 1671. [CJR#434]

**DE GRAVE,** master George Wells, from Newfoundland via
Barbados to Cadiz, Spain, in 1699. [SPAWI.1699/1007]

**DE GRIFFOEN,** [The Griffin], 280 tons, from the Netherlands
to the Nieuw Nederland in 1625. [NMM]

**DE GROEN VOET,** [The Green Foot], a Dutch ship captured
by the English at Barbados in 1655. [SPAWI.1655/1979]

**DE GROENE ARENT,** [The Green Eagle], from Holland in
May 1659 to Curacao, arrived in New Amstel, the Nieuw
Nederland, on 11 August 166o bound for Amsterdam,
Holland, sailed on 30 August 1660. [PA.2.7/646, 648]

**DE GROOTE CHRISTOFFEL,** [The Great Christopher],
from Amsterdam, Holland, to the Nieuw Nederland in
1654. [NMM]

**DE GROOTE GERRIT,** [The Great Gerrit], 300 tons, master
Paulus Leendertszoon van der Grift, from the
Netherlands to the Nieuw Nederland *with passengers* in
August 1646 via Curacao, arrived in May 1647.
[GAA.NA#1340][DNY#1/455]

**DE GROOTE MANE,** [The Great Moon], from Texel in

North Holland on 8 August 1618 bound via the Straits of Magellan to the Moluccas. [HS.2$^{nd}$ series.XVIII]

**DE GROOTE SONNE,** [The Great Sun], from Texel in North Holland on 8 August 1618 bound via the Straits of . Magellan to the Moluccas. [HS.2$^{nd}$ series, XVIII]

**DE GRUENVROUW,** [The Green Wife], master Nicolaes Boes, at Ferryland, Newfoundland, 1673. [NA.CO1.34.37/85]

**DE GULDEN ARENT,** [The Golden Eagle], master Jacob Jansen Staats, from the Netherlands *with 5 passengers* in January 1661, arrived in the Nieuw Nederland by 2 June 1661 from the Netherlands, from there on 21 July 1661 to the Netherlands; master Pieter Claeszoon Deugt, to the Nieuw Nederland *with 8 passengers* in January 1662; ? from Amsterdam bound for New Amstel on the South (Delaware) River, the Nieuw Nederland, *with passengers* on 11 March 1662. [CJR#254][NYCol.ms#14/83-123] [DNY#2/452][HH#166][NWI.I.194][DH.VIII.310]

**DE GULDEN BEVER,** [The Golden Beaver], from the Nieuw Nederlands bound for Holland in October 1658. [CJR#127]

**DE GULDEN LEEUW,** [The Golden Lion], master Frans Adriaenszoon Speck, from the Netherlands to Pernambuco in 1600. [GAR.ONA.7.46.143; 7.9.22]

**DE GULDEN LEEUW,** [The Golden Lion], from the West Indies to the Netherlands in 1633. [GAR.ONA/321/139/340]

**DE GULDEN LEEUW VAN VLAANDEREN,** [The Golden Lion of Flanders], master Nathaniel Jesson, from Amsterdam, Holland, in August 1651, bound for Virginia, arrived there in October 1651. [NA.HCA.Exams.Vol.66]

**DE GULDEN LEEUW VAN SORDAM,** [The Golden Lion of Sordam], master Burgh Jacobs, from Surinam in

October 1674 bound for Amsterdam, Holland, was
captured by a French privateer, The Golden Fleece, in
December 1674 and taken to France. [SPAWI.1677/593,
581][ActsPCCol.1676/1093]

**DE GULDEN STER,** [The Golden Star], was captured at
Barbados by the English in 1655. [SPAWI.1655/1979]

**DE GULDEN WOLF,** [The Golden Wolf], a Dutch West
Indies Company ship which was captured by the English
in 1638. [SPAWI.1699/1101]

**DE GULDEN ZONNE,** [The Golden Sun], master Francis
Wier, at Curacao in January 1677; seized by pirates off
Carthagena in 1677. [DI.I/244][SPAWI.1679/867, 1331]
[PCCol.1679/1242]

**DE HAAS,** [The Hare], a Dutch vessel captured by the English
at Barbados in 1655. [SPAWI.1655/1979]

**DE HAAS VAN MEMBLICKE,** [The Hare of Memblicke],
master Henrik Cornellisson, to Barbados, Martinique and
St Eustatia in 16..

**DE HARTOGH VAN JORCK,** [The Duke of York], master
Pieter Reyerszoon, from Amsterdam, Holland, in
February 1668 bound for Nieuw Amsterdam, from there
in July 1668 bound for the Netherlands; from Holland in
April 1669 bound for New York; master Johannes
Luyck, from the Netherlands to New York, arrived there
in September 1670.
[CJR#398/400/421][CMR#9][NMM]

**DE HASE,** from Middelburg, Zealand, to Guyana in 1600.
[ARA.SG.RGP#85/343]

**DE HONDT VAN VLISSINGEN,** [The Dog of Flushing],
from the Netherlands to Newfoundland in 1615.
[NA.HCA.14/41.9]

**DE HOOP VAN AMSTERDAM,** [The Hope of Amsterdam],
from the Netherlands to the Amazon in 1604; master
John Sims, from the Netherlands to the Amazon in 1605.

[HS.2$^{nd}$ series, 171/27]; from Guina via England to the Netherlands in 1606. [HS.2$^{nd}$ series, 56/lxix]

**DE HOOP,** [The Hope], from the Netherlands to St John's, Witless Bay, Cape Broyle and Aquafort, Newfoundland in 1626. [GAA.NA.256/349]

**DE HOOP VAN MIDDELBURG,** [The Hope of Middelburg], master Leonard Corneliszoon, a privateer, seized the St Domingo off Florida, but when returning to the Netherlands was captured and taken to Dublin, Ireland, around 1636. [NA.HCA.13.53.91]

**DE HOOP,** [The Hope], master Jan Jans Ramasijn, from the Maas, Zealand, to Madeira in 1637; in the West Indies, 1639; master Jan Tjebkenszoon, to the Nieuw Nederland in 1643; at Barbados and St Kitts in 1646; master Jan Aelbertss Kas, at Barbados and St Kitts in 1647. [GAR.ONA.259.58.103/302.333.668/ 96.144.232] [GAA#2224]

**DE HOOP,** [The Hope], master Job Aertsen, from Virginia to the Netherlands in 1647. [GAR.ONA.475.124.182]

**DE HOOP,** [The Hope], master Adriaen Blommart, from the Netherlands to the Nieuw Nederland in 1657, and return in October 1657; master Pieter Amilius, to the Nieuw Nederland *with passengers* in April 1660; master Pieter Amilius, from the Netherlands *with 72 passengers* in January 1661 bound for the Nieuw Nederland, from there in June 1661 bound for the Netherlands; master Pieter Amilius, from the Netherlands *with 73 passengers* in April 1660; arrived in the Nieuw Nederland in April 1662, from Nieuw Amsterdam on 6 September 1662 bound for Holland. [CJR#65/254/297/301][GAA#2224] [DNY#2/452][HH#166][NYCol.mss#14/83-123]

**DE HOOP,** [The Hope], master Adrian Jacobsen, from Brandenburg, Germany, to the Danish West Indies in May 1688. [RAK]

**DE HOOP VAN AMSTERDAM,** [Hope of Amsterdam], master John Swan, at Barbados in March 1678. [St Michael's burial register]

**DE HOOP CASTEEL VAN SLUYS,** [The Hope Castle of Sluys], from Rotterdam, Zealand, to Barbados to St Kitts then Virginia and return to Rotterdam, but was captured by pirates off Ostend, Flanders, in 1647. [GAR: 31.1.1648]

**DE HOOP WEL,** [The Hope Well], from Nieuw Amsterdam to the Netherlands in August 1666. [CJR#388]

**DE IJSSERDRAADVAT,** [The Wire-barrel], from Holland *with 22 passengers* to the Nieuw Nederland in 1657. [HH#166]

**DE JACOB,** [The James], 200 tons, from Rotterdam, Zealand, to Newfoundland to Pernambuco to St Kitts to Virginia, and return in 1642. [GAR.ONA.8/6/1642]

**DE JAGER,** [The Hunter], from Texel in the Netherlands on 8 August 1618 bound via the Straits of Magellan to the Moluccas. [HS.2$^{nd}$ series.XVIII]

**DE JAGER VAN ROTTERDAM,** [The Hunter of Rotterdam], arrived in the Netherlands from Brazil and Tortuga in 1635. [GAR.ONA.167.73.129]

**DE JAGER,** [The Hunter], from Pernambuco bound for the Netherlands in 1640. [GAR.ONA.86.171.305]

**DE JAGER,** [The Hunter], from Amsterdam, Holland, bound for the Nieuw Nederland in 1646. [NMM]

**DE JONGE BONTECOE,** [The Young Spotted Cow]. master Jan Ryckertsen, at Curacao in October 1659. [DI.I/146]

**DE JONGE JAN,** [The Young John], from Middleburg, Zealand to Essequibo in April 1700, arrived there on 8 July 1700, returned to Middleburg in May 1701. [SWAWI.1700/715; 1701/303, 416]

**DE JONGE PRINS VAN DEENEMARCKEN,** [The Young Prince of Denmark], from Amsterdam, Holland, bound for the Nieuw Nederland in 1648. [NMM]

**DE JONGE TOBIAS,** [The Young Tobias], master Thijs Voilckertszoon Mossel, from Monnikendam, the Netherlands, bound for the Hudson River in 1612 and return in 1613. [GAA][NNC#22]

**DE KAT VAN HOLLAND,** [The Cat of Holland], 200 tons, from La Rochelle via Dieppe, France, *with 155 passengers* bound for Quebec on 27 April 1665, arrived there on 18 June 1665. [La Rochelle archives][Archives de la Charente Maritime #B5665/10]

**DE KLEIN LAM VAN HOORN,** [The Little Lamb of Hoorn], 160 tons, from La Rochelle, France, *with a passenger* to Quebec in 1667. [La Rochelle Archives, Teuleron #100]

**DE KOCK,** [The Cock], from Amsterdam, Holland, to the Nieuw Nederland in 1661. [NMM]

**DE KONING BALTHAZAR,** [The King Balthasar], master Jan Erasmus Reining, at Curacao and the West Indies in 1690.

**DE KONINGH CAREL,** [The King Charles], master Jan Jansz Beste Vaer, from the Texel, Netherlands, in April 1668 bound for Nieuw Amsterdam, returned from there in August 1668. [CJR#408/412][PCCol.1668/496]

**DE LA VICTOIRE,** [The Victory], master Urbain de Roissey, from Le Havre, France, *with passengers* bound for St Kitts and Barbados in 1627. [HCF.I.392][TA#118]

**DE LEEUWINNE,** [The Lioness], master Jan Pietersz, from Vlissinghen, Zealand, on 22 January 1627 bound via the Canary Islands to the Amazon, arrived there on 7 March 1627. [HS.2$^{nd}$ series.171/269]

**DE LIEFDE,** [The Love], master Marten Cael, from Texel, Holland, *with passengers* bound for the Nieuw

Nederland on 25 September 1638, arrived in Nieuw
Amsterdam on 27 December 1638; master Meindert
Janszoon Schellinger, from the Netherlands *with
passengers* bound for Pernambuco and St Kitts in 1640;
at Barbados, 1640.arrived in the Nieuw Nederland *with
passengers* in 1655; master Jan Adriaenszoon Crul, *with
passengers* to the Nieuw Nederland in March 1660;
master Claes Jansz de Wit, from Amsterdam to the
Nieuw Nederland in September 1660.
[GAR.ONA.86.198.365] [NY.Col.MS#14] [PA.2/7/482,
631][CJR#235][GAR.ONA.86.198.365; 138.422.645]

**DE LIEFDE,** [The Love], a Dutch prize, taken at Barbados in
1655. [SPAWI.1655/1979]

**DE LIEFDE,** [The Love], master Jeroen Jeroensen, to Virginia
in 1675. [PCCol.1675/2]

**DE LIEFDE,** [The Love], master Theophile Thomas, from
Brandenburg, Germany, to the Danish West Indies in
May 1688. [RAK]

**DE LUYPAERT,** from the Netherlands to Newfoundland in
1658. [GAA.NA1539/187-8]

**DE MACKREEL VAN VLISSINGEN,** [The Mackerel of
Flushing], a 60 ton yacht, master Pieter Janszoon, from
Flushing in the Netherlands *with Walloon settlers* to the
Amazon in 1623. [HS.2nd series, 171/258]
[BL.Sloan.ms.179b, ff 2, 2v]

**DE MACKREEL,** [The Mackerel], from Texel, Holland, on
16 July 1623 bound for the Hudson River, returned in
1624; *with 42 passengers* bound for the Nieuw
Nederland in 1625. [Algemeen Rijksarchief, #5751]

**DE MAECHT VAN DORDRECHT,** [The Power of
Dordrecht], in the West Indies, 1632.
[GAR.ONA.286.97.127]

**DE MAECHT VAN ENCHUYSEN,** [The Power of
Enchuysen], master Laurens Corneliszoon, from the

Netherlands to the Nieuw Nederland before 1650. [DNY#I/431]

**DE MAECHT VAN MEDENBLIK,** [The Power of Medenblik], from the Netherlands to Bahia in 1639. [GAR.ONA.200.3.03]

**DE MARGRIET,** [The Margaret], arrived in New York in October 1680 from the Netherlands. [CMR#40]

**DE MEERMAN,** [The Merman], master Jan Janszoon Bezstevaer, from Amsterdam, Holland, to New Oranje in 1674. [NMM]

**DE MEEUWE VAN AMSTERDAM,** [The Seagull of Amsterdam], from Texel in the Netherlands on 8 August 1618 bound via the Straits of Magellan to the Moluccas. [HS.2$^{nd}$ series, XVIII]

**DE MELCKMEYT,** [The Milkmaid], from Amsterdam, Holland, bound for the Nieuw Nederland in 1642. [NMM]

**DE MEULEN,** [The Mill], from Amsterdam, Holland, in April 1657 bound for New Amstel in the Nieuw Nederland, [Delaware], *with 108 passengers*, arrived there on 27 September 1657; from Nieuw Amsterdam in the Nieuw Nederland bound for Bordeaux, France, in 1659. [CJR#166][NYSA.NYCM.18.47][DNY#2/20, 50] [PA.2.7/553]

**DE MOESMAN,** [The Market Gardener], master Jacob Janszoon Staedt, from Amsterdam, Holland, *with 6 passengers* bound for the Nieuw Nederland in May 1658; from Nieuw Amsterdam bound for the Netherlands in October 1658; master Jacon Janszoon Staedt, from Amsterdam *with 23 passengers* bound for the Nieuw Nederland in April 1659, from there on 5 September 1659 return; to the Nieuw Nederland *with 32 passengers* on 9 March 1660, from the Nieuw Nederland to the Netherlands in August 1660. [CJR#111/236] [HH#166] [PA.2.7/597][NYCol.MS.Vol.14/86/10][SI]

**DE MORGEN SLAAF VAN HOLLAND,** [The Morning
Slave of Holland], master Abraham Leonardson, was
wrecked on an island off Jamaica in May 1697.
[SPAWI.1699/1353]

**DE MORGENSTAR,** [The Morning Star], from Texel in the
Netherlands on 8 August 1618 bound via the Straits of
Magellan to the Moluccas. [HA.2$^{nd}$ series, XVIII]

**DE MORGENSTERRE VAN MIDDELBURCH,** [The
Morningstar of Middleburgh], in the West Indies, 1641.
[GAR.ONA.306.52.83]

**DE MOUTON,** [The Sheep], from France to Canada in June
1677. [BN.Trompeur#174/395]

**DE NACHTEGAAL,** [The Nightingale], master Thijs Mossel
or Volckertssen, from the Netherlands to the Nieuw
Nederland in 1613. [DNY#1.11]

**DE NEPTUNUS,** [The Neptune], master Maerten
Willemszoon, from the West Indies to the Netherlands in
1600; from the West Indies bound for the Netherlands in
1628. [GAR.ONA.8.121.399; 84.481.121]

**DE NEPTUYNIS,** [The Neptune], a yacht, from the
Netherlands to Curacao by 1644. [DNY#1/165]

**DE NIEU AMSTERDAM,** [The Nieuw Amsterdam], from
Amsterdam, Holland, to Nieuw Amsterdam in 1655.
[NMM]

**DE NIEU JORCK,** [The New York], from the Netherlands to
New York in April 1683. [CMR#100/102/104]

**DE NIEU NEDERLANDT,** [The Nieuw Netherlands], master
Cornelis Jacobsen May, from Holland in March 1623,
arrived in the Mauritus River, (Hudson River), in May
1623; from the Netherlands via England to St Vincent
and St Kitts in 1631. [VDC]

**DE NIEU NEDERLANDT FORTUYN,** [The New
Netherland Fortune], master Daniel Michielsen, from

Amsterdam, Hollands, via Rhode Island, to Nieuw
Amsterdam in 1655. [DNY#1/324]

**DE ONRUST,** [Restless], master Cornelius Hendrickson, from
Monnickedam in the Netherlands, arrived at the South
(Delaware) River in 1616. [NNC#35]

**DE ORANGE VAN NIEUDAM,** [The Orange of Nieudam],
master Valck Claessen, from La Rochelle, France, to
Quebec in 1667. [La Rochelle Archives, Teuleron#88]

**DE ORANGEBOOM VAN AMSTERDAM,** from the
Netherlands via Plymouth bound for America in 1625.
[PCCol.1625/133]

**DE ORANGEBOOM,** [The Orange Bush], master Cornelis
Pietersz. Puyt, from St Kitts to the Netherlands in 1647;
master Willem Harmensen, from Virginia to the
Netherlands in 1649. [GAR.ONA.87.22.43; 87.139.266]

**DE ORANGEBOOM VAN MIDDLEBURG,** [The Orange
Bush of Middleburg], from St Kitts bound for the
Netherlands when captured by a Portuguese privateer
and taken to Plymouth, England, in 1662.
[PCCol.1662/575]

**DE ORANGIENBOOM,** [The Orange Bush], from Brazil to
Dordrecht, the Netherlands, in 1624; master Jan
Alewijns, from the Maas, the Netherlands, to
Pernambuco in 1632; from the West Indies to the
Netherlands in 1633.
[GAR.ONA.156.23.46/144.169.361/322.7.14]

**D'ORANJE BOOM,** [The Orange Bush], from Nieuw
Amsterdam to the Netherlands in July 1667. [CJR#391]

**DE OTTER,** [The Otter], master Cornelis Reyers van der
Beets from Amsterdam, Holland, on 17 February 1659
*with passengers* bound for the South River settlement of
the Nieuw Netherlands; to the Nieuw Netherlands *with
passengers* in April 1660. [CJR#313][PA.2.7/557]
[NY.Col.MSS.13/106; 14/97]

**DE OUD SIMEON VAN DURKERDAM,** [The Old Simeon of Durkerdam], 200 tons, master Simon Doridod, from La Rochelle, France, *with soldiers* bound for Quebec in 1665. [La Rochelle Archives]

**DE PAEREL,** [The Pearl], arrived in Nieuw Amsterdam on 6 August 1661, and returned to the Netherlands on 18 October 1661; arrived in New York in July 1684 from the Netherlands. [CJR#260][CMR#155]

**DE PAROQUIT,** [The Parakeet], a yacht or bark, from the Netherlands to Curacao by 1664. [DNY#1/165]

**DE PAUWE,** [The Peacock], from Amsterdam, Holland, bound for the Nieuw Nederland in 1642. [NMM]

**DE PEREBOOM,** [The Peartree], from the Netherlands *with passengers* bound for the Nieuw Nederland in 1654. [NYCol.ms#14/83-123]

**DE PIJNAPPEL,** [The Pineapple], from Amsterdam, Holland, in 1648 bound for the Nieuw Nederland. [NMM]

**DE POOSTHOORN,** [The Posthorn], from Amsterdam, Holland, to New York in 1668. [NMM][GAA#2845]

**DE PRISE DE ST MARTIN DE RE,** 100 tons, master Josue Boutin, from France to Quebec in 1688. [Gironde archives B72/163]

**DE PROFEET DANIEL VAN AMSTERDAM,** [The Prophet Daniel of Amsterdam], from the Netherlands to Newfoundland and return via Italy in 1656. [GAA.NA2117/89-91]

**DE RENSSELAERWIJK,** master Jan Tjepkeszoon Schellinger, from Texel, Holland, on 1 October 1636 *with 35 passengers* bound for Rensselaerwijk in the Nieuw Nederland, arrived there on 4 March 1637. [GAA#1045][SI]

**DE ROMEYN,** [The Roman], master Dirck Claeszoon Boot, from Amsterdam, Holland, to the Nieuw Nederland in 1652. [NWI.1.126]

**DE ROODE LEEUW,** [The Red Lion], master Dirck Willems Pastoor, from Amsterdam, Holland, via Iberia and the Canary Islands to Brazil in 1597. [GAA.NA.76/208]

**DE ROODE ROOSEBOOM,** [The Red Rosebush], master Pieter Reyersz, from Amsterdam , Holland,to the Nieuw Nederland in March 1663. [CJR#314]

**DE ROOSE,** [The Rose], master Pieter Symonsz., from Virginia to the Netherlands in 1648. [GAR.ONA.87.99.196]

**DE ROOSEBOOM,** [The Rose Bush], master Pieter Reyerszoon Van Der Beets, from the Netherlands to the Nieuw Nederland *with 75 passengers* on 15 March 1663; from the Nieuw Nederland to Amsterdam, Holland, in August 1663; from Nieuw Amsterdam on 17 August 1664 bound for the Netherlands. [DNY#2/232, 466][SI] [HH#166][NYCol.ms#14/83-123]

**DE RUIJTER,** [The Cavalier], 260 tons, when bound from Amsterdam, Holland, via the West Indies to the Nieuw Nederland in 1625, was captured by Moorish pirates off the coast of Africa. [GAA#652]

**DE ST JACOB,** [The St James], from the Netherlands to the Nieuw Nederland *with 3 passengers* in 1663. [NYCol.ms#14/83-123]

**DE ST JAN BAPTIST,** [The St John the Baptist], master Symon Claesen, from the Netherlands bound *with passengers* for the Nieuw Nederland in 1657, arrived there on 23 December 1657; master Jane Bergen, to the Nieuw Nederland *with 50 passengers* in May 1661. [NYCol.ms#14/83-123]

**DE ST PIETER,** [The St Peter], master Jacob Jacobszoon, from the Netherlands to the Nieuw Nederland *with 8 passengers* in October 1663. [NYCol.ms#14/83-123]

**DE SALM,** [The Salmon], a yacht, from Texel, Holland, *with passengers* bound for the Nieuw Nederland in December 1630. [VDV#108-135]

**DE SALM VAN DORT,** [The Salmon of Dort], master Barent Nanningszoon, at St Kitts and Barbados in 1644. [GAR.ONA.114.141.236]

**DE SAMPSON,** [The Sampson], master Adriaen Sampson, from West Indies to the Netherlands, wrecked on the coast of Wales in 1603. [GAR.ONA.10.56.173]

**DE SAYER,** from Brazil bound for the Netherlands in 1643. [GAR.ONA.82.4.15]

**DE SCHAEP,** [The Sheep], 200 tons, from the Netherlands *with passengers* to the Nieuw Nederland in 1625. [GAA#226]

**DE SCHILDPAD,** [The Tortoise], master ... Eelckens, from Amsterdam, Holland, to America in 1616. [GAA.NA#645/36-43]

**DE SCHILT,** [The Shield], from the Netherlands to the Nieuw Nederland in 1618. [DNY#1/21]

**DE SCHOTSEN DUYTSMAN,** [The Scots Dutchman], master Jacob Eversen Sandelijn, from Amsterdam, Holland, to Nya Sverige, (New Sweden), in 1646. [NMM]

**DE SEVENSTER,** [The Seven Stars], from the Nieuw Nederland to the Netherlands on 15 September 1635; master Jan Claeszoon, from Amsterdam, Holland, bound for Nieuw Amsterdam in 1642. [VDV][NMM]

**DE SIEBEN PROVINCIEN,** [The Seven Provinces], from Brandenburg, Germany, to St Thomas, Virgin Islands, in March 1698. [RAK]

**DE SONNE,** [The Sun], from Amsterdam, Holland, to the South (Delaware) River in 1658. [DNY#2/60]

**DESPATCH,** a brigantine, master Andrew Gibson, from Leith, Scotland, bound for Darien, Panama, but wrecked off Islay, Scotland, in February 1699. [NAS.GD406]

**DE STATYN,** master Isaacq Gerritszoon Schaep, from the Netherlands on 27 September 1663 *with 46 to 52 passengers* bound for the Nieuw Nederland; from Nieuw Amsterdam on 23 April 1664 bound for the Netherlands. [CJR#336][DNY#2/234, 468][NYCol.ms#14/83-123] [SI][HH#166]

**DE STER,** [The Star], master Claes Floriszoon, from the Netherlands *with 3 passengers* bound for the Nieuw Nederland in Jun 1663; arrived in Nieuw Amsterdam on 18 September 1664 from the Netherlands. [NYCol.mss#14/83-123][DNY#2/466]

**DE STERRE VAN AMSTERDAM,** [The Star of Amsterdam], master Claes Bret, from Virginia and the Nieuw Nederland, via Jersey in the Channel Islands, to London arriving on 18 September 1664. [DNY#2/254]

**DE STUYVESANTS WAPEN,** [The Arms of Stuyvesant], from Nieuw Amsterdam in the Nieuw Nederland on 11 September 1662 bound for the Netherlands. [DNY#2/462]

**DE SWAEN,** from Brazil bound for the Netherlands in 1642; master Aryaen Hendricksz., from Delftshaven, the Netherlands, bound via Rouen, France, to St Paulo, Pernambuco, in 1643. [GAR.ONA.81.350.1089/ 82.4.15]

**DE SWANENBURGH,** master Evert Corneliszoon, from Vlissingen, Netherlands, to New York in 1673. [NMM]

**DE SWARTE ARENT,** [The Black Eagle], to the Nieuw Nederland in 1655. [NYSA.NYCM#12/17]

**DE SWARTE BEER,** [The Black Bear], master Hendrick Christiaenszoon, from Amsterdam, Holland, bound for the Nieuw Nederland in October 1618, arrived at the

Hudson River in 1619, from there to Zealand.
[GAA#645][NNC#36/54][RAC#38]

**DE SWARTE PAERT,** [The Black Horse], to the Nieuw
Nederland in 1625. [GAA#226]

**DE SWARTE RAAF,** [The Black Raven], from Amsterdam,
Holland, in 1643 bound for the Nieuw Nederland.
[NMM]

**DE SWOLL,** to the Nieuw Nederland in 1643; at Curacao in
1645. [DNY#1/165]

**DE SYV PROVINCIER,** [The Seven Provinces], master
Albert von der Lain, from Brandenburg, Germany, to St
Thomas, Virgin Islands, in November 1692. [RAK]

**DE TARRUW SCHUUF,** master James Conway, from
Virginia to the Netherlands in 1662.
[GAR.ONA.235.40.78]

**DE TIJGER,** [The Tiger], master Adriaen Block, to the Nieuw
Nederland in October 1613, arrived in the Hudson River
in 1614. [DNY#1/11]

**DE TIJGER,** [The Tiger], master Pieter Walings, in the West
Indies and Brazil, 1628; master Leunis Pieterszoon, at
Barbados in 1630; in the West Indies, 1632.
[GAR.ONA.141.40.212;163.8.10;286.1.1; 304.226.298]

**DE TORTELDUYFKEN,** [The Turtle Dove], in the West
Indies, 1634. [GAR.ONA.97.200]

**DE TROUW,** [The Faithful], from Amsterdam, Holland, to
Newfoundland in 1658; master Jan Janszoon Bestevaer,
from the Netherlands *with 98 passengers* bound for the
Nieuw Nederland in February 1659; from Nieuw
Amsterdam in July 1659 bound for the Netherlands;
master Jan Janszoon Bestevaer, *with 60 passengers*
bound for the Nieuw Nederland in December 1660; from
the Nieuw Nederland on 18 July 1661 bound for the
Netherlands; master Jan Janszoon Bestevaer, bound for
the Nieuw Nederland *with 27 passengers* in March 1662;

from Nieuw Amsterdam on 6 September 1662 bound for Holland; master Jan Janszoon Bestevaer, bound for the Nieuw Nederland *with 17 passengers* in January 1664; from the Nieuw Nederland in July 1664 bound for the Netherlands. [CJR#217/229/297/362][DNY#2/60, 454] [NYCol.ms#14/56, 83-123][PA.2.7/649] [GAA.NA2711/963]

**DE VALK,** [The Falcon], from the West Indies to the Netherlands in 1628, [GAR.ONA.84.487.135]; master Gerrit Jansz., at Sint Maartens, West Indies, in September 1631. [VDV]

**DE VALKENIER,** [The Falconer], 160 lasts, master Willem Thomassen, from Amsterdam, Holland, *with 140 passengers* bound for the Nieuw Nederland in 1650; from Amsterdam to the Nieuw Nederland in March 1656. [DNY#1/376][GAA#1345/1298]

**DE VERGULDE BEER,** [The Golden Bear], master Jan Jansen Bestevaer, from the Nieuw Nederland to Holland in November (?) 1655; from Nieuw Amsterdam in June 1657 bound for Holland; master Cornelis Willemsen de Beer, from the Netherlands in December 1657 bound for the Nieuw Nederland; master Cornelis Willemse de Beer, from the Nieuw Nederland to the Netherlands in July 1658; from Nieuw Amsterdam to the Netherlands on 18 October 1661. [CJR#19/48/68/104/264]

**DE VERGULDE BEVER,** [The Golden Beaver], master Jan Reyerszoon van der Beets, from the Netherlands *with passengers* to the Nieuw Nederland in 1658; from the Netherlands to the Nieuw Nederland in 1659; from the Netherlands *with passengers* to the Nieuw Nederland in 1660. [CJR#150][NYCol.mss#14/83-123]

**DE VERGULDE DOLPHIJN,** [The Golden Dolphin], master Jacob Centen, from the West Indies and Virginia to the Netherlands in 1662. [GAR.ONA.231.217.385]

**DE VERGULDE ENGEL,** [The Golden Angel], from Dutch Brazil to the West Indies then Virginia and return to the Netherlands in 1650. [GAA.NA.1589/387]

**DE VERGULDE KOCK VAN VLISSINGEN,** [The Golden Cock of Flushing], master Pieter Adriaenszoon, from the Netherlands to the Amazon in 1616 and return in 1618. [Bodleian Library, Oxford, Rawlinson ms#A175, ff370-1][HS, series II, Vol.171/163]

**DE VERGULDE MEULEN,** [The Golden Mill], master Barent Jochemsz, from the Nieuw Nederland to the Netherlands in September 1657; arrived at Fort Altena in the Nieuw Nederland *with passengers* in 1659. [CJR#61/73][PA.2.7/623]

**DE VERGULDE OTTER,** [The Golden Otter], from Amsterdam, Holland, *with passengers* to the Nieuw Nederland in summer (?) 1656; master Jan Janszoon Bestevaer, from the Netherlands *with 3 passengers* to the Nieuw Nederland on 22 December 1657; master Cornelis Reyerszoon van de Beets, from the Netherlands to the Nieuw Nederland *with 38 passengers* in 1658, and similarly *with 56 passengers* in 1660. [CJR#193] [NYCol.ms#14/83-123, 84/8][HH#166]

**DE VERGULDE SCHEL,** [The Golden Shell], master Adriaen Blommaeet, from Holland to the Nieuw Nederland in 1654. [NWI.I.123]

**DE VERGULDE SONNE,** [The Golden Sun], from the South (Delaware) River to Amsterdam, Holland, in 1658; master Adolf Wyngaert, from Nieuw Amsterdam in the Nieuw Nederland to Amsterdam, Holland, in June 1658. [DNY#2/49, 61]

**DE VERGULDE STAR,** [The Golden Star], from Amsterdam, Holland, in June 1663 bound for the Nieuw Nederland. [DNY#2/230]

**DE VISSCHER,** [The Fisher], at Nieuw Amsterdam in 1653, also in August 1659. [RNA#1/66][CJR#166]

**DE VLIEGENDE DRAECK,** [The Flying Dragon], 45 lasts, master Geleyn van Stapels, from the Netherlands *with passengers* bound for the Amazon in 1624-1625, arrived in the Wiapoco on 23 May 1625 from the Amazon; master Galeyn van Stapels, from Flushing (Vlissingen) in the Netherlands on 22 January 1627 bound via the Canary Islands and the coast of Africa to the Amazon, arrived there on 3 March 1627 [HS.2nd series, 171/80, 269]

**DE VLIEGENDE HART,** [The Flying Heart], master Jan Alewijn Coel, from the Netherlands to Curacao and Tortuga in 1635. [GAR.ONA.150.527.837]

**DE VLIEGENDE PARD VAN VLISSINGEN,** [The Flying Horse of Flushing], from Virginia to the Amazon in 1615. [HS.2nd series.171.47][HMC, 4th Report, appx.469]

**DE VLIEGENDE PARD,** [The Flying Horse], master Juriaen Aernoutsz, from Curacao via New York to Acadia in 1674. [DCB.I.39]

**DE VLIEGENDE VIS VAN VLISSINGEN,** [The Flying Fish of Flushing], arrived in Virginia on 20 December 1625. [RVC.IV.567]

**DE VOGELSANGH,** [The Birdsong], master Jacob Jansoon Staas, arrived in Nieuw Amsterdam, Nieuw Nederland, on 18 June 1657 from the Netherlands; from Nieuw Amsterdam in August 1657 bound for the Netherlands. [CJR#50/56][NMM]

**DE VOGEL STRUYS,** [The Ostrich], master Symen Cornelis Gilde, from Curacao, in July 1657, via the Nieuw Nederland, in September 1657, to the Netherlands. [CJR#62][DI#I/138]

**DE VOORLOPER,** [The Forerunner], from the Nieuw Nederland via Barbados to the Netherlands in October 1650. [DNY#1/447]

**DE VOS,** [The Fox], master Jan Corneliszoon May, from Amsterdam, Holland, to New France in 1611-1612.

**DE VOS,** [The Fox], master Jacob Janszoon Huys, from the Netherlands to the Nieuw Nederland *with 44 passengers*

in August 1662, arrived there on 14 November 1662;
returned to the Netherlands on 7 January 1663.
[NYCol.ms#14/83-123][DNY#2/462, 464]

DE VOSJE, [The Little Fox], master Pieter Franszoon, from
Amsterdam, Holland, to the Nieuw Nederland in 1614.
[NNC#30]

DE VREDE VAN AMSTERDAM, [The Peace of
Amsterdam], master John Oxford, from Amsterdam,
Holland, to Virginia and return in 1654-1655.
[SPAWI.1654/30]

DE VREDE, [The Peace], a Dutch prize, taken at Barbados in
1655. [SPAWI.1655/1979]

DE VREEDE, at Caplin Bay, Newfoundland, in 1659.
[GAA.NA2715/509]

DE VRUNTSCHAP, master James Woodcock, at St Kitts and
Barbados in 1644. [GAR.ONA.86.307.585]

DE WAEGH, [The Scales], from Amsterdam, Holland, bound
for Fort Casimir on the South River, [Delaware], in
1654; master Frederic de Cominck, from Amsterdam to
the Nieuw Nederland in 1655; master Hendrick de Raet,
from Amsterdam *with 17 passengers* bound for the
South River on 27 May 1657, from Nieuw Amsterdam to
the Netherlands in October 1657. [DNY#1/583; 2/20]
[CJR#65]

DE WALVIS, [The Whale], master Pieter Hayes, from Texel,
Holland, *with 30 passengers* bound for Tortuga on 12
December 1630; arrived there but, as existing colony had
been destroyed, moved north to Nya Sverige, (New
Sweden), landed at Lewes Creek, and settled at
Zwaanendael. [HDC.II.2][VDV#108-135]

DE WASBLEECKER, [The Bleacher], to the Nieuw
Nederland in 1653; master Aert Cosijns, was sunk near
Martinique when bound for the Nieuw Nederland in
1657. [GAA.NA#2860/200; inv.541; NA#2880/80]

**DE WEST FRIESLAND VAN HOORN,** [The West
Friesland of Hoorn], master John Johnson, from Port
Royal, Jamaica, to Holland in February 1669.
[SPAWI.1669/21]

**DE WESTINDISCHE RAVEN,** [The West Indian Raven],
master Cornelis Pieterszoon, from Amsterdam, the
Netherlands, to Nieuw Amsterdam in 1638. [NMM]

**DE WEYMANSGENEUCHT,** from Virginia to the
Netherlands in 1646. [GAR.ONA.208.36.45]

**DE WILLEM,** [The William], master Jacon Eelkes, arrived in
Nieuw Amsterdam in the Nieuw Nederland from the
Netherlands via London in 1633. [GAA#1400]

**DE WITTE DOFFER,** [The White Dove], master Willem
Janssen Houton, from Amsterdam, Holland, to Virginia
in 1621. [DNY#1/26]

**DE WITTE DOFFER,** [The White Dove], from the
Netherlands to the Nieuw Nederland in 1646.
[GAA#817]

**DE WITTE ENGEL,** [The White Angel], master Jacob
Lauwer Van Slot, from Virginia to Amsterdam, Holland,
on 6 June 1659, but was captured by a warship from San
Sebastien, Spain. [CLRO]

**DE WITTE HONDT,** [The White Dog], master Claes
Henryckzoon, from Hoorn in the Netherlands via Lisbon
to Brazil in the 1590s. [RAC#24]

**DE WITTE KLOODT,** [The White Ball], master Dirck
Mooninck, from Amsterdam, Holland, to New York in
1671. [NMM]

**DE WITTE LEEUW,** [The White Lion], from Amsterdam,
Holland, to New France in 1606. [SH#8]

**DE WITTE LEEUW,** [The White Lion], Captain Jaap, arrived
at Point Comfort, Virginia, from the West Indies in
August 1619. [WMQ.54.392] [RVC.III.243]

**DE WITTE SWAEN VAN DELFT,** [The White Swan of Delft], in the West Indies, 1638. [GAR.ONA.293.113.136]

**DE WITTE SWAEN,** [The White Swan], in the West Indies, 1642. [GAR.ONA.307.55.82]

**DE WITTE VALCK,** [The White Falcon], master Willem Dircksen, from Amsterdam, Holland, in October 1641 bound for the Nieuw Nederland, arrived in Nieuw Amsterdam in November 1641. [NMM]

**DE WITTEN WINTHONT,** [The White Greyhound], master Barent Nannings, at St Kitts and the West Indies, 1634. [GAR.ONA.322.193.449; 94.21.40]

**DE YONGE JAN,** [The Young John], from Middelburg, Zealand, in April 1700 bound for Essequibo, arrived before 9 August 1700. [SPAWI.1700.715]

**DE ZEE FORTUYN VAN SCHIEDAM,** [The Sea Fortune of Schiedam], trading in St Kitts and Nevis during 1655. [NA.Inter-Regnum Entry Book, Vol.CII/706-725]

**DE ZEELAND,** [The Zealand], from Zealand to Guiana, arrived there in February 1667. [HS.2$^{nd}$ series.56/207]

**DE ZEELANDT,** [The Zealand], in the West Indies, 1635. [GAR.ONA.302.194.402]

**DE ZEERIDDER,** [The Knight of the Sea], from the Netherlands to Trinidad and the Wild Coast in 1598. [ARA.SG.12563/3]

**DE ZEEROP,** from the Netherlands to Brazil in 1636. [GAR.ONA.167.150.246]

**DE ZWAAN,** [The Swan], from Middelburg, Zealand, to the West Indies in 1629. [GAR/ONA/189/182/300]

**DE ZWEMMENDE LEEUW,** [The Swimming Lion], master Gillis Dornhoven, from Zealand to the West Indies and return in 1595. [AZ.Minutes of the State of Zealand, 11.3.1595]

**DEN AEOLUS VAN VLISSINGHEN, ZEELAND,** [The Aeolus of Flushing],master Job Cornelissen, from Texel, Holland, on 8 August 1618 bound via the Straits of Magellan to the Moluccas. [HS.2$^{nd}$ series.XVIII]

**DEN CALMAR SLEUTEL,** [The Key of Kalmar], master Jan Hendrickxzoon van de Waetter, from Texel, Holland, in December 1637 *with 6 passengers* bound for Rensselaerwijk, Nieuw Nederland. [NMM]

**DEN CONINCK DAVID VAN ENKHUIZEN,** from the Netherlands to Newfoundland in the mid-1620s. [GAA.NA]

**DEN CONINCK DAVID,** [The King David], master David de Vries, 14 guns, 25 crew, and *30 planters*, from Hoorn and Texel, Holland, on 10 July 1634 bound for Guiana, landed there on 14 September 1634, from there in December 1634 via the West Indies to the Nieuw Nederland, arrived at Fort Amsterdam on 1 June 1635, from there to the Netherlands on 15 September 1635; master Job Arissen, from Amsterdam, Holland, *with 7 passengers* bound for the Nieuw Nederland on 23 July 1641, arrived in Nieuw Amsterdam on 29 November 1641, similarly in 1642 and 1643; from Amsterdam to Newfoundland in 1651; possibly captured by the English at Barbados in 1655. [VDV][SPAWI.1655/1979] [HH][SI][GAA.NA1534/277]

**DEN CONINCK SALOMON,** [The King Solomon], at Nieuw Amsterdam in June 1654 bound for the Netherlands; from Amsterdam, Holland, via Guinea to Curacao, arrived there on 2 July 1659, from there to the Netherlands. [DI.I/140][NYCol.ms#17/41]

**DEN CRONEDE GRIF,** master Cornelius Krisen, from Denmark to the West Indies in September 1675; master Johen Blom, from Copenhagen, Denmark, to St Thomas in the Virgin Islands in June 1680. [RAK][DWI]

**DEN ENGELL GABRIELL,** [The Angel Gabriel], from the Netherlands to Brazil in 1633. [GAR.ONA.256.211.336]

**DEN EYCKEBOOM,** [The Oaktree], from Amsterdam, Holland, *with 41 passengers* bound for the Nieuw Nederland on 17 May 1641, arrived there in August 1641; arrived in Curacao in 1659; from Manhattan to the Netherlands in October 1660; from the Netherlands in December 1662 bound for the Nieuw Nederland; from the Nieuw Nederland in May 1663 bound for Amsterdam; from Nieuw Amsterdam on 26 May 1664 bound for the Netherlands. [DI.I/149][CJR#239/316] [DNY#2/232, 465]

**DEN GOUDEN LEEUW,** [The Golden Lion], master Frans Adriaensz. Speck, to Pernambuco, Brazil, in 1600. [GAR.ONA.78.201.406]

**DEN GOUDEN LEEUW,** [The Golden Lion], master Pieter Cornelisz. Doncker, arrived in the Netherlands from Brazil in 1635. [GAR.ONA.167.159]

**DEN HARINCK,** [The Herring], master Symen Dirckszen, from Texel, Holland, on 7 September 1637 *with 4 passengers* bound for Nieuw Amsterdam, arrived there on 28 March 1638; from Texel in May 1638 *with 19 passengers* bound for the Nieuw Nederland, arrived in Nieuw Amsterdam on 14 August 1638; from Texel *with passengers* bound for the Nieuw Nederland in May 1639, arrived in Nieuw Amsterdam on 7 July 1639. [NWI.I.119][GAA#1420]

**DEN HOLLANDSCHEN TUYN,** [The Dutch Garden], from Brazil to the Netherlands in 1638. [GAR.ONA.86.109.198]

**DEN HOUTTYN,** [The Wooden], master Adriaen Dircksen, from Texel, Holland, *with passengers* in June 1642 bound for the Nieuw Nederland, arrived in Nieuw Amsterdam on 4 August 1642. [VRB]

**DEN LEEUWINNE,** [The Lioness], 100 lasts, master Jan Pieterszoon, from Flushing in the Netherlands, on 22

January 1627 bound, via the Canary Islands and the coast
of Africa, to the Amazon, arrived there on 3 March 1627.
[Hakluyt#2/171/269]

**DEN OTTER,** [The Otter], master Pieter Jansz Aemilius, from
Amsterdam, Holland, to the Nieuw Nederland in June
1656, arrived in Nieuw Amsterdam on 5 September
1656, from Nieuw Amsterdam in November 1656 bound
for the Netherlands but was wrecked off the coast of
England. [CJR#28/29/30]

**DEN OUDE WAGEN,** [The Old Wagon], from Amsterdam,
Holland, in May 1664 bound for the Nieuw Nederland.
[NMM]

**DEN PAON VAN VENELOO,** [The Peacock of Venlo],
master Andre Chaviteau, from La Rochelle, France, *with
passengers* to Quebec in 1666. [La Rochelle Archives,
Teuleron and Savia ms]

**DEN PHOENIX VAN VLISSINGEN,** [The Phoenix of
Flushing], 200 tons, master Johan Bosseman, from La
Rochelle, France, *with passengers* to Quebec in 1663.
[La Rochelle Library, Moreau ms; La Rochelle Archives,
Teuleron ms]

**DEN PROPHETTE SALOMON,** [The Prophet Solomon],
master Jan Jacobs Vosch, from Madeira to the
Netherlands in 1643. [GAR.ONA.95.178.289]

**DEN PURMERLANDER KERCK,** [The Church of
Purmerland], master Dierck Jacobszoon Vries, from
Texel, Holland, to New Amstel in the Nieuw Nederland
*with passengers* on 27 November 1661, arrived at the
South River (Delaware) on 3 March 1662; from Nieuw
Amsterdam, on 5 June 1662 bound for Amsterdam;
master Benjamin Barentszoon, from the Netherlands in
October 1662 bound for the Nieuw Nederland, arrived
there *with 48 passengers* on 29 March 1662; from Nieuw
Amsterdam to the Netherlands in May 1663; from
Amsterdam in September 1663 *with passengers* bound
via the South River settlement (Delaware) to Nieuw
Amsterdam in the Nieuw Nederland, arrived on 18

February 1664, from there to the Netherlands on 12 May 1664. [CJR#293/294/322][NYGBR.LX/60,68-70] [NYCol.ms#14/83-123][DNY.2/191, 454][NWI.I.194] [PA.2.7/673, 678, 710.714]

**DEN RODE HANE,** [The Red Cock], from Copenhagen, Denmark, to St Thomas in November 1687, arrived there on 23 February 1688. [DWI]

**DEN SOUTBERG,** [The Salt Mountain], from the Netherlands to the Nieuw Nederland in 1631; from Texel, Holland, in July 1632 *with 32 passengers* bound via Sint Maartens, in the West Indies, for Renselaerwijk in the Nieuw Nederland, arrived at Fort Amsterdam in the Nieuw Nederland in April 1633. [VDV][VRB#807] [GAA.91/915]

**DEN SPIEGEL,** [The Looking Glass], was captured by the English off Maryland in 1643; master Havicke Corleisen Cocke, from Rotterdam, Zealand, to Virginia in 1644. [NA.HCA#13/60][Md.Hist.Mag]

**DEN TIJGER,** [The Tiger], from the Netherlands to Brazil in 1639; in the West Indies, 1642. [GAR.ONA.262.302.490/308.59.80]

**DEN WATERHONDT,** [The Water Dog], from Barbados to Amsterdam, Holland, and Hamburg, Germany, in 1638; from Texel, Holland, *with 13 passengers* bound for Rensselaerwijck, Nieuw Nederland, in July 1640, arrived there in October 1640. [VRB#822]

**DEUX FRERES DE BORDEAUX,** [The Two Brothers of Bordeaux], 300 tons, master Jean Bonfils, from France to Quebec in 1695. [Gironde Archives,6B76/103.117]

**DEUX SOUERS DE LA ROCHELLE,** [The Two Sisters of La Rochelle], 180 tons, master Pierre Chaveau, from France to Canada and the West Indies in 1684. [NA.HCA.32/181]

**DIAMANT DE BORDEAUX,** [The Diamond of Bordeaux], 130 tons, master Jacques Jentel, from France to Canada during 1690. [Gironde Archives 6B74/48, B295]

**DIAMOND,** from France to Newfoundland in 1696. [BN.Collection Clairambault, #277/153]

**DIANE,** master Jean Masson, from La Rochelle, France, to Quebec in 1675. [Charente Maritime ms#B5674]

**DIE BRACKE,** master Cornelius de Clercq, from Brandenburg, Germany, to St Thomas, Virgin Islands, in December 1692. [RAK]

**DIE BURG VON STADEN,** [The Burgh of Staden], trading with Virginia or Barbados in 1674. [PCCol.1674/1006]

**DIE KONINGEN VON SCHWEDEN VON STADT,** [The Queen of Sweden of Stadt], trading with Virginia or Barbados in 1674. [PCCol.1674/1006]

**DIE VIER BRUDER,** from Brandenburg, Germany, to St Thomas, Virgin Islands, in March 1698. [RAK]

**DIEMEN,** from Amsterdam, Holland, bound for the Nieuw Nederland in September 1658. [DNY#14/439]

**DILIGENTE DE LA ROCHELLE,** [The Speedy of La Rochelle], 200 tons, master Andre Chaviteau, from La Rochelle, France, to Quebec during 1683; master Jean Du Rand, from La Rochelle *with passengers* to Quebec and the West Indies in 1685; master Du Rand, from La Rochelle to Chedabouctou in 1686; master Du Rand, from La Rochelle to Quebec in 1687 and also in 1688. [Gironde Archives #B72/158; Charente Maritime Archives B5681/83/85; La Rochelle Archives; BN. Collection Arnoul #21443]

**DOLPHIN,** from Boston via Newfoundland and the Orkney Islands, Scotland, to Holland in June 1680. [JJD]

**DOLPHIN OF BOSTON,** a pink, master Alexander McCall, arrived in Glasgow, Scotland, on 20 July 1686 from

Virginia; from Glasgow on 30 August 1686 to Madeira; master Michael Shuite, from Boston, New England, to Amsterdam, Holland, in September 1693. [NAS.E72.19.12; GD1.885.2/2; RH15.106.801]

**DOLPHIN OF NEW YORK,** 35 tons, master William Baker, from Holland via the Isle of Wight, England, bound for New York in 1692. [ActsPCCol.1692#364/120; 467/3]

**DOLPHIN OF LIVERPOOL,** master William Benn, from Dublin, Ireland, in April 1697 bound for Antigua. [NA.HCA.Exams.Vol.81]

**DOLPHIN,** master John Malloch, from Leith, Scotland, on 14 July 1698 *with passengers* bound for Darien on the Isthmus of Panama. [NAS.GD406, b.C23/3, b.161, 25/23]

**DON DE DIEU,** from St Malo, France, to Newfoundland in 1599 and 1600; master Henri Couillart, from Honfleur, France, to Tadoussac on the St Lawrence River in 1602; from Honfleur, France, in 1600 bound for Tadoussac; master Samuel de Champlain, from Honfleur in April 1608 to the St Lawrence River. [BNF#64/67/68/93][DCB.I.209]

**DON DE DIEU,** from Quebec to France in August 1631; master Pierre Morielt, arrived in Quebec on 22 May 1633. [DCB.I.159][NAC]

**DORDRECHT,** arrived in the Netherlands from Brazil and the West Indies in 1624; master Nicolaes Verhauzen, from the Netherlands to the West Indies and Brazil in 1632. [GAR.ONA.156.16.31/129.91.282/166.88.154]

**DORFLING,** master Abraham Meelter, from Brandenburg, Germany, to St Thomas in the Virgin Islands in March 1691. [RAK]

**DOROTHEA,** master Louis de Visser, from Denmark to St Thomas in the Virgin Islands, in September 1687. [RAK]

**DOROTHY,** a Brandenburg vessel, Captain Balopin, arrived in Weymouth, England, in 1689 from the West Indies. [ActsPCCol.1689/332]

**DORT,** master Cornelis Pieterszoon, in the West Indies, 1634. [GAR.ONA.302.98.202]

**DOVE OF BOSTON, NEW ENGLAND,** master Nicholas Skinner, from Amsterdam, Holland, to Boston, New England, in 1675. [GAA.NA.3222/387]

**DRAGON OF LEITH,** from Leith, Scotland, bound for Greenland, 1678-1685. [NAS.GD18.2568/2570]

**DRAGON DE LA ROCHELLE,** [The Dragon of La Rochelle], 80 tons, master Nicolas Noel, from La Rochelle, France, to Quebec and the West Indies in 1688. [Charente Maritime archives #235/168]

**DRAGON,** 120 tons, master Nicholas Young, with a crew of eight men, from Cork, Ireland, to Carbonear, Newfoundland, in 1698. [IJMH#12/1/52]

**DRAGON,** arrived in Acadia on 5 September 1699 from France. [ASC#120]

**DUBLIN,** a 150 ton pink, master John Goulding, with a crew of 25 men, from Dublin, Ireland, to St John's, Newfoundland, in 1679; from Dublin to Bay Verde, Newfoundland, in 1681. [NA.CO1/47, 113/121; CO1/46, 33/4]

**DUBLIN MERCHANT,** from Belfast, Ireland, to Barbados and the West Indies in 1679; master Robert Ross, at Middlesex County, Virginia, in August 1699. [BMF#180][ACV]

**DUE RETURN OF LYNN,** 60 tons, master Simon Tuchin, from Ireland via Madeira and Dominica to Virginia in 1625. [NA.1/111#34]

**DUFVAN,** from Sweden to Nya Sverige, (New Sweden), in 1638. [SSD#120]

**DUKE OF HAMILTON,** master Walter Duncan, from the River Clyde, Scotland, *with passengers* to Darien on the Isthmus of Panama on 18 August 1699, from there *with passengers* to South Carolina, wrecked in Charleston Bay in August 1700. [NAS.CC8.8.83]

**DUKE OF YORK,** master Johannes Luyck, from Amsterdam, Holland, via England to New York in 1670. [GAA#2223]

**EAGLE,** 120 tons, master Ninian Barclay, from London, England, to Dunbarton, Scotland, in March 1627, from there *with passengers* to Nova Scotia in 1627; master William Ramsay, from Dunbarton *with passengers* to Nova Scotia in 1628. [Dunbarton Burgh Records]

**EAGLE OF PERTH,** master George Ferguson, from Perth, Scotland, bound for Virginia in 1681. [RCRB.IV.570]

**EAGLEWING,** 150 tons, from Carrickfergus, Ireland, *with 140 passengers* bound for Massachusetts on 9 September 1636, returned to port, storm-damaged, on 3 November 1636. [JSIS#1/1/1-18]

**EDMUND OF MONTSERRAT,** from Montserrat to Galway, Ireland, in 1673. [Blake Family Records, 1600-1700, {London, 1905},#173]

**EDWARD OF BRISTOL,** master John Scott, from Ireland *with passengers* to Barbados in 1654. [NA.HCA.Libels #112/195]

**ELBINCK,** from Amsterdam, Holland, to Nieuw Amsterdam, Nieuw Nederland, in 1652. [NMM]

**ELECTORAL PRINCE,** arrived in St Thomas, West Indies, on 7 March 1690. [DWI]

**ELEFANTEN,** [The Elephant], master Jens Munk, from Copenhagen, Denmark, on 9 May 1619 bound for the North West Passage. [RAK]

**ELIZABETH,** master John May, from Barbados bound for Kinsale, Ireland, arrived in Waterford, Ireland, on 31 October 1637. [NA.HCA.13/54/490]

**ELIZABETH DE DIEPPE,** [Elizabeth of Dieppe], master James Le Bas, a Huguenot, from the French Plantations in the West Indies and Barbados bound for France, when captured by the frigate <u>Dragon</u> and taken to Weymouth, England, in 1654. [SPCol.XII.28]

**ELIZABETH,** a Dutch prize, taken at Barbados in 1655. [SPAWI.1655/1979]

**ELIZABETH OF LIMERICK,** master John Morgan, at Jamaica in September 1661. [SPAWI.1661/169]

**ELIZABETH OF LEITH,** master Andrew Spankie, from Leith, Scotland, *with passengers* bound for Virginia in 1667. [RPCS.II.358]

**ELIZABETH OF JERSEY,** from Boston, New England, to Jersey in the Channel Islands in 1677. [ActsPCCol.1677/1182]

**ELIZABETH DE LA ROCHELLE,** [Elizabeth of La Rochelle], from France to Quebec in 1689; from France to Canada and the West Indies in 1692; master Michel Camouin, possibly to Quebec in 1698. [La Rochelle library #3E1858/21; Charente Maritime Archives #B5687/8; B5694]

**ELIZABETH,** master Thomas Shadwick, arrived in Port Glasgow, Scotland, on 2 July 1691 from Virginia. [NAS.E72.15.21]

**ELIZABETH OF BERWICK,** probably from Scotland to New York in 1693. [NYD.IV.354]

**ELIZABETH AND KATHERINE,** from Scotland to Virginia in 1678. [NAS.RH9.8.229]

**EMIRILLON,** from La Rochelle, France, to Canada in August 1684, arrived in Rochefort, France, in 1685 from Canada. [BN.Collection Arnoul#21331/21443]

**ENDEAVOUR OF CORK,** master John Knight, from Montserrat to Galway, Ireland, in 1675. [Blake family Records, #176, {London, 1906}]

**ENDEAVOUR OF LIVERPOOL,** master Andrew Dalbord, from Port Glasgow, Scotland, to New England in September 1684. [NAS.E72.19.9]

**ENDEAVOUR OF CHARLESTOWN, NEW ENGLAND,** master John Brakenbury, from Port Glasgow, Scotland, to the West Indies in November 1688; arrived in Port Glasgow on 20 July 1689 from Nevis; from Port Glasgow to Madeira in September 1689. [NAS.E72.19.14/15]

**ENDEAVOUR OF GLASGOW,** master Peter Hunckin, arrived in Port Glasgow, Scotland, on 24 August 1691 from New England. [NAS.E72.15.21]

**ENDEAVOUR,** master John Anderson, from Leith, Scotland, *with passengers* bound for Darien on the Isthmus of Panama on 14 July 1698. [NAS.GD406.b161, 25/5]

**ENHIORHINGEN,** [The Unicorn], master Jens Ericksen Munk, from Copenhagen, Denmark, to Hudson Bay on 9 May 1619, arrived there on 7 September 1619, returned to Norway on 26 June 1620, landed there on 21 September 1620. [DCN.I.515]

**ENTREPRENANT,** [Enterprising], from La Rochelle, France, to Canada in August 1684. [BN.Collection Arnoul#21443]

**ENVIEUX,** [Envious], from France to Quebec in 1692; master Simon Pierre Denys, arrived in Acadia in June 1695 from France; Captain Iberville, from Rochefort, France, in July 1696 bound for Quebec. [ASC#165/180]

**ERASMUS,** master Jacob Eeuwontsz, in the West Indies, 1634; from the Netherlands to Brazil in 1635. [GAR.ONA.302.87.181/99.77.150]

**ERASMUS VAN ROTTERDAM,** from Brazil bound for the Netherlands in 1643. [GAR.ONA.82.4.15]

**ESPERANCE,** from Honfleur, France, to Newfoundland in 1597; Captain Guyon-Dieres, from Honfleur to Tadoussac on the St Lawrence River in 1601 and in 1602; from Honfleur, France, in 1600 bound for Tadoussac. [DCB.I.209][BNF#64/67]

**ESPERANCE,** [Hope], 90 tons, master Savinien Courpon de la Tour, arrived at Tadoussac, Canada, on 30 June 1640; master H. L'Angevin, arrived in Quebec during July 1642; Admiral S. Courpon de la Tour, arrived in Quebec during August 1643. [NAC]

**ESPERANCE,** [Hope], master Jean Masson, from La Rochelle, France, to Quebec in 1669; from La Rochelle to Canada in 1671; from France to Canada in June 1677. [Charente Maritime Archives B5669][WMQ.LII.82] [BN.Melange de Colbert #174/395]

**ESPERANCE,** [Hope], from Marseilles, France, on 12 March 1687 *with 100 Huguenot passengers* bound for Martinique, shipwrecked off the island on 19 May 1687 when *37 passengers* were drowned. [HEA#226]

**ESPERANCE DE FLESSINGUE,** [The Hope of Flushing], from La Rochelle, France, to Placentia, Newfoundland, in 1696. [BN.Collection Clairmabault.277/153]

**ESTHER OF DUBLIN,** seized by HMS Dartmouth and tried before the Admiralty Court at Nevis in April 1686. [SPAWI.1686/621]

**ESTOILE DU JOUR,** master Claude Le Clerc, from France to Quebec in 1695. [Charente Maritime Archives B235/336]

**ESTOURNEAU,** from Dieppe, France, on 28 April 1628 *with passengers* bound for Canada. [DCB.I.579]

**ETHELRED,** master Nicholas French, from London via Galway, Ireland, bound for Barbados in 1696, captured by French privateers and taken to Martinique. [NA.Exams.Vol.81]

**EWE AND LAMB,** master John Guthrie, from Leith, Scotland, in January 1667 *with passengers* bound for Virginia; from Leith to Virginia in 1668; from Leith to Virginia in 1669; from Leith *with passengers* to Virginia in February 1670; from Leith *with passengers* to the American Plantations in May 1672; from Leith *with passengers* in February 1679; from Leith *with passengers* to Virginia in August 1683. [RPCS.II.201/446; III.198/523/650][NAS.E72.15.12/16]

**EXCHANGE OF STOCKTON,** master James Peacock, from Leith and Aberdeen, Scotland, *with 31 passengers* to East New Jersey on 10 August 1683, arrived at Staten Island, New York, on 19 December 1683. [NAS.E72.1.10]

**EXPECTATION OF BOSTON,** a 180 ton pink, Captain Grecian, arrived in Boston, New England, in May 1680 from Cork, Ireland. [SPAWI.1680/1374]

**EXPRESS OF LONDON,** master William Pickman, arrived in Leith, Scotland, in September 1666 from Barbados. [NAS.E72.15.2]

**FAEROE,** [Pharaoh], from Copenhagen, Denmark, on 1 October 1671 *with 77 passengers* bound for St Thomas in the Virgin Islands, [RAK]

**FALCON,** arrived in St Thomas, West Indies, on 24 November 1686. [DWI]

**FAMA,** master Peter Pawelson Kabeliaw, from Gothenburg, Sweden, *with passengers,* bound via the Canary Islands and Antigua to Nya Sverige, (New Sweden), on 16 August 1642, arrived at Fort Christina on 15 February

1643; from Nya Sverige, (New Sweden), via St Kitts in
1644 bound for Harlingen in the Netherlands.
[PMH.II.326][SSC#760][DNY#1/143]

**FAME OF LIVERPOOL,** master John Glover, arrived in
Glasgow, Scotland, on 2 March 1689 from Virginia.
[NAS.E72.19.14]

**FAMILLE DE LA ROCHELLE,** [The Family of La
Rochelle], master Jean Garesche, from France to Quebec
and Newfoundland in 1691. [Charente Maritime
Archives B5687/88]

**FARNAMBURKE,** a Dutch ship which was captured at
Barbados in 1655. [SPAWI.1655/1679]

**FELLOWSHIP,** 45 tons, master William Whitness, with a
crew of 7 men, from Waterford, Ireland, to St John's,
Newfoundland, in 1679. [NA.CO1/43/202]

**FERO,** from Bergen, Norway, *with passengers* bound for St
Thomas in the Virgin Islands, arrived there on 25 May
1672. [DWI]

**FIDELITY OF WATERORD,** master J. Richards, at
Ferryland, Newfoundland, in 1701. [MUN]

**FILLE BIEN AYMEE DE LA ROCHELLE,** [The Good Girl
Aymee of La Rochelle], master Jean Duret, from France
to Quebec and the West Indies in 1693. [Charente
Maritime Archives B5687/8]

**FLEUR DE LYS,** [The Lily Flower], 50 tons, master Jean
Barjaut, from France to Quebec in 1688. [Gironde
Archives 6B72/60]

**FLEUR DE MAI CHAILLEVETTE,** [The Mayflower of
Chaillevette], master Jean Morgat, from La Rochelle,
France, to Quebec in 1690. [Charente Maritime Archives
B235]

**FLUTE ROYALE DE BROUAGE,** [The Royal Flute of
Brouage], master J. Guillon, from La Rochelle, France,

*with passengers* bound for Quebec in 1662. [NAC] [La Rochelle library, Moreau]

**FOGEL GRIPEN,** [The Bird Griffin], a sloop, master Andrian Joransen or Jacob Barben, from Stockholm, Sweden, *with 30 passengers* to Nya Sverige, (New Sweden), in August 1637, arrived in April 1638, from there in April 1639 bound via St Kitts to Gothenburg, Sweden, arrived there in June 1639. [SSD#758][SD#30-33]

**FORT ALBANY OF NEW YORK,** from Amsterdam, Holland, *with passengers* bound for New York in 1669. [SPAWI.1669/32]

**FORTUNA,** arrived in St Thomas in the Virgin Islands on 13 October 1684, from there on 31 March 1685 bound for Copenhagen, Denmark, from Copenhagen on 15 October 1685 bound via Nevis for St Thomas, arrived there on 24 February 1686. [DWI]

**FORTUNE OF WEXFORD,** from St Kitts in February 1638 bound for Kinsale, Ireland. [NA.HCA.13/54/281]

**FORTUNE OF WATERFORD,** possibly to Virginia 1669. [PCCol.1669/851]

**FORTUNE,** 100 tons, master Pierre Le Besson, arrived in Quebec in 1654; master Elie Raymond, arrived in Quebec in 1655; arrived in Quebec in 1656. [NAC]

**FORTUNE VAN ENKHUISEN,** [The Fortune of Enkhuisen], sank off Barbados in 1655. [SPAWI. 1655/219]

**FORTUNE,** from Nantes, France, to Guadaloupe in 1665, captured by the English off Bermuda on its return voyage. [ActsPCCol.1668/739]

**FORTUNE OF DUBLIN,** 90 tons, master Robert Holmes, from Ireland to Antigua in 1696, captured by a French privateer and taken to Martinique, later ransomed and taken to Antigua in August 1696. [NA.AC13.Vols.81-82:13.4.1698][SPAWI.1698/431iv]

**FORTUNE BLANCHE DE AMSTERDAM,** [White Fortune of Amsterdam], master Pierre Gaigneur, from La Rochelle, France, to Quebec in 1666. [La Rochelle library Teuleron 93]

**FORTUNE DOREE,** [The Golden Fortune], 140 tons, master Francois Janot, arrived in Quebec in 1662. [NAC]

**FORTUYN VAN HOORN,** [The Fortune of Hoorn], master Hendrick Christiaenseb, from Hoorn, Holland, to the Nieuw Nederland in 1613; master Cornelius Jacobssen Mey, from the Netherlands to the South (Delaware) River in 1614. [NNC#22][DNY#1/11]

**FORTUYN,** master Willem Willems Moy, from Barbados to the Netherlands in 1644. [GAR.ONA.248.103.198]

**FORTUYN,** [Fortune], a Dutch Prize, captured by the English at Barbados in 1655. [SPAWI.1655/1979]

**FORTUYN VON HAMBURG,** a galliot, master Derrick Dieters, arrived in Martinique during 1667. [SPAWI.1667/1502]

**FOURGON,** from France *with passengers* to Canada in 1685. [BN.Collection Arnoul]

**FRANCIS,** 80 tons, master Robert Hanford, with a crew of 22 men, from Waterford, Ireland, to Fermeuse, Newfoundland, in 1676. [NA.CO1/38.223]

**FRANCIS,** 67 tons, with a crew of 12 men, from Waterford, Ireland, to St John's, Newfoundland, in 1679. [NA.CO1/43.202]

**FRANCIS,** 50 tons, master John Langdon, with a crew of 4 men, from Youghal, Ireland, to St John's, Newfoundland, in 1679. [NA.CO1/43.202]

**FRANCIS,** 70 tons, master Samuel Morgan, with a crew of 13 men, from Limerick, Ireland, to St John's, Newfoundland, in 1680. [NA.CO1/46.33]

**FRANCOIS DE HAVRE DE GRACE,** [Francis of Havre de Grace], Captain Regnold, from St Kitts and Barbados, taken by the English in 1629-1630. [Cal.SPCol.V.111]

**FRANCOISE,** [Frances], master Jean Girot, from Rouen, France, *with passengers* to Ile de Sable in 1598; master Jean Girot, from Honfleur, France, bound for Tadoussac on the St Lawrence River on 15 March 1603, arrived there on 26 May 1603. [DCB.I.421] [BNF#74/76]

**FRANCOISE,** [Frances], master Thomas Poittevin, arrived in Quebec during 1676. [NAC]

**FREDERICK OF NEW YORK,** 60 tons, master Humphrey Perkins, from Delaware Bay and New York to Amsterdam, Holland, and Hamburg, Germany, in 1698, arrived there on 27 June 1698, returned to New York. [NA.HCA.Exams.Vol.81][SPAWI.1698/794]

**FREDERICK IV,** from Denmark via Guinea to St Thomas, Virgin Islands, arrived there in October 1700. [DWI]

**FRIDERICH DER DRITTE,** master Jacob Lambrecht, from Emden, Germany, via Guinea to St Thomas in 1696; master Wouter Ypes, from Brandenburg to St Thomas, Virgin Islands, in March 1698. [DWI][RAK]

**FRIDERICH WILHELMUS,** master Jean Le Sage, from Brandenburg, Germany, to St Thomas, Virgin Islands, in March 1692. [RAK]

**FRIENDS ADVENTURE OF GLASGOW,** master Mark Hawking, arrived in Glasgow, Scotland, on 7 September 1686 from Virginia; from Glasgow to New England in October 1686. [NAS.E72.19.12]

**FRIENDS ADVENTURE OF NEW YORK,** a 40 ton sloop, master Edward Barber, from Scotland *with 50 passengers* via Barbados to Virginia in 1698. [NA.CO33/13]

**FRIENDSHIP,** 70 tons, with a crew of 10 men, from Waterford, Ireland, to the Bay of Bulls, Newfoundland, in 1679; master Richard Dandridge, from Waterford to Newfoundland in 1680. [NA.CO1/43.202; CO1/46.26]

**FRIENDSHIP OF GLASGOW,** master Joseph Hardy, arrived in Port Glasgow, Scotland, from Virginia in March 1681; from Port Glasgow to New England on 16 April 1681; master John McColl, returned to Port Glasgow from New England in December 1681; from Port Glasgow to Boston, New England, on 27 February 1682. [NAS.E72.19.1/2/5]

**FRIENDSHIP OF BOSTON,** a brigantine, master Thomas Eyre, arrived in Port Glasgow, Scotland, on 15 August 1691 from America; master Henry Hill, arrived in Leith, Scotland, in July 1696 from Boston, New England. [NAS.E72.19.21; GD1.885.23]

**FRIENDSHIP,** from Dublin, Ireland, *with passengers* bound for Jamaica in 1695. [ActsPCCol.1695/577iv]

**FRIENDSHIP OF BELFAST,** 60 tons, master Hans Hammell, from Belfast, Ireland, to America, arrived in the Rappahannock River, Virginia, in April 1699, also in August 1699; captured by pirates off the coast of Virginia in 1700. [NA.CO5/1441; HCA.A/26, 14]

**FUCHS,** to St Thomas, Virgin Islands, in 1690. [DWI]

**FULWOOD,** a ketch, master Nathaniel Davis, arrived in Port Glasgow, Scotland, in July 1682, from Virginia. [NAS.E72.19.5]

**GASTON,** 100 tons, master G. Joubert, arrived in Quebec in June 1641. [PAC]

**GECROONDE LIEFDE,** master Jan Janssen Poont, from Pernambuco and St Kitts to the Netherlands in 1646. [GAR.ONA.87.22.43]

**GEDEON,** [Gideon], from France to Canada in 1670. [BN.Melanges de Colbert]

**GELDERIA,** master Cornelis Janz. Niels, arrived at Sint
Maartens in the West Indies in September 1631. [VDV]

**GENT,** in the West Indies, 1640. [GAR.ONA.301.78.166]

**GEORGE OF GREENOCK,** from Greenock, Scotland, *with
passengers* to Carolina in 1686. ['Early Annals of
Greenock', Greenock, 1905]

**GIDEON,** master Simon Cornelissen Gilde, from Curacao via
the Caribbee Islands to Amsterdam, Holland, in 1659;
master Simon Cornelissen Gilde, from Curacao via the
Caribbee Islands to Amsterdam in 1660; master Simon
Cornellissen Gilde, from Amsterdam to Nieuw
Amsterdam in 1663; master Simon Gilde van Baarop,
from Manhattan in the Nieuw Nederland to Amsterdam
in 1664. [DI.I/150][NYCol.mss#17/57][DNY#2/744]

**GIFT OF AYR,** master Thomas Megonin (?), in Barbados,
1655. [Minutes of the Council of Barbados, #i/91]

**GIFT OF GOD OF GUERNSEY,** master Eli Nichols, was
seized by the colonial authorities in Boston, New
England, in 1680. [ActsPCCol.1681/44]

**GLASGOW MERCHANT,** master George Dredan, from
Glasgow, Scotland, *with passengers* bound for the West
Indies in 1670; returned to Glasgow on 20 October 1670
from Nevis. [RPCS#3/259][NAS.E72.10.3]

**GLORIEUX,** from France to Cayenne in 1676. [DCB.I.63]

**GLORIEUX DE BORDEAUX,** [Pride of Bordeaux], master
Louis de Harismendy, from France *with passengers*
bound for Quebec and Newfoundland in 1690. [Gironde
Archives]

**GOLDEN CROWN,** master Arent Henricksen, from Denmark
to St Thomas in the West Indies on 30 August 1671.
[DWI]

**GOLDEN HORSE,** from Ireland *with passengers* to Virginia
in 1653. [NA.Inter-regnum Entry Book #98/405]

**GOLDEN HYND OF LONDON,** from Aberdeen, Scotland, *with passengers* to West New Jersey on 4 July 1682, arrived in the Delaware River during October 1682. [NAS.E72.1.7][History of PA.#i/60, Philadelphia, 1797]

**GOLDEN LYON OF DUNDEE,** master Thomas Auchenleck, from Dundee, Scotland, via London to Virginia in 1627. [NA.E190.31.1]

**GOLINTH ST THOMAS,** from Denmark to the West Indies in December 1673. [RAK]

**GOOD FAME,** from New York via London, England, to Amsterdam, Holland, in 1670. [GAA#3205/4003]

**GOODFELLOW OF BOSTON,** master George Dell, from Kinsale, Ireland, *with passengers* to the Rappahannock River, Virginia, in December 1653; master George Dell, arrived in New England in May 1654 *with passengers* from Ireland. [NA.Inter-Regnum Entry Book #98/338] [Cal. SPCol.vol.XII.407] [NA.Libels#112/107, 131] [Essex County Quarterly Court Records, Vol.II]

**GOOD HOPE OF BOSTON,** master Robert Wallace, from Port Glasgow, Scotland, to New England in April 1683, and returned via Barbados in July 1683; master Richard Smith, from Port Glasgow to New England in February 1685. [NAS.E72.19.8/9]

**GOOD INTENT,** master John Scott, from Leith, Scotland, to Virginia or Barbados in 1667. [RPCS.II.358]

**GOOD INTENTION OF GALWAY,** at Antigua in 1687. [Acts PCCol.1687/221]

**GORDOMAN PHOENIX,** master John Gordon, from Scotland to Charles Island, Nova Scotia, in 1627. [NAS.AC7.1.184]

**GRACE DE DIEU,** [Grace of God], master Charles Biencourt de Saint Just, from Dieppe, France, *with 36 passengers* bound for Port Royal, Acadia, on 26 January 1611,

landed there on 22 May 1611; from France *with
passengers* on 13 March 1613, arrived at Port Royal in
May 1613. [DCB.I.67/98/100]

**GRACE OF KIRKCUDBRIGHT,** (Gordon of Lochinvar's
ship), to America after 8 October 1626. [DBR:Kenmure
Charter Chest]

**GRACE OF GOD OF DUNDEE** master William Lindsay,
from Lisbon, Portugal, to Newfoundland in 1600.
[SHS.Misc.X]

**GRAND CARDINAL,** a 200 ton frigate, from France to
Acadia in 1645. [DCB.I.505]

**GRAND CERF,** master Pierre Lebon, from Le Havre, France,
to Perce, Quebec, 1654. [DCB.I.115]

**GREAT HOPE OF BOSTON,** master Robert Wallace,
arrived in Glasgow during July 1683 from Barbados.
[NAS.E72.19.8]

**GRENADE DE LA ROCHELLE,** [The Pomegranate of La
Rochelle], master Thomas Pruneau, from France to
Quebec in 1698. [Gironde Archives ms 6B298/B5694]

**GYLDEN LOVE,** [Golden Lion], master Johan Vinck, from
Denmark to St Thomas, Virgin Islands, in March 1698.
[RAK]

**GYLDEN LOVES VAABEN,** [Arms of the Golden Lion],
from St Thomas in the Danish West Indies to Bergen,
Norway, and Copenhagen, Denmark, in 1692; master
John Johnson, from Denmark to the West Indies in 1693.
[RAK.West Indian Archives #174][SPAWI.1698/404ii]

**HAABET,** [Hope], master Peder Erichsen Hensing, from
Denmark to St Thomas in the Virgin Islands in
November 1689.[RAK]

**HAFMANDEN,** [Merman], a frigate bound for the Danish
West Indies, 28 February 1674, arrived in St Thomas, the
Virgin Islands, *with passengers* on 12 May 1675;

returned in 1676; master Jan Blom, from Copenhagen, Denmark, on 6 November 1682 *with passengers* bound via the Azores for St Thomas in the Virgin Islands. [RAK][IJMH.II/2/103][DWI]

**HALVE MAEN,** [Half Moon], 80 tons, master Henry Hudson, from Holland on 6 April 1609, arrived at the North River, the Nieuw Netherlands, on 2 September 1609. [DNY#1/275]

**HANNAH OF CORK,** a brig, from Jamaica to Cork in 1705. [CalSPDom.SP63/365/127]

**HANNAH AND SARAH,** master John Carter, from Rotterdam, Zealand, to Boston, New England, in September 1686. [NAS.GD1.885.2/1]

**HAPPY RETURN,** master William Measure, from Rotterdam, Zealand, to New York in 1687. [GAA.NA.3292/152]

**HAPPY RETURN,** master George Duncan, from Scotland on 28 September 1698 *with passengers* bound for Barbados, arrived there on 11 December 1698, returned to Scotland via Newfoundland. [NAS.RH15.101.3]

**HARCOURT,** from France to Newfoundland in 1696. [B.N.Collection Clairambault, 277/153]

**HARMAN DE TRAMLADE,** master Jacques Chevalier, from Newfoundland bound for France when captured by the Dutch and taken to Plymouth, England, in 1673. [ActsPCCol.#975]

**HAVRE DE FLESSINGUE,** [Harbor of Flushing], 100 tons, master Andre Chaviteau, from La Rochelle, France, to Quebec in 1670. [WMQ.LII.96][Charente Maritime Archives, msB5669]

**HELENE VAN VLISSINGEN,** [Helen of Flushing], 100 tons, master Andre Chaviteau, from La Rochelle, France, to Quebec in 1670. [Archives de la Charante Maritime, 30.4.1672]

**HELPWELL,** master John Greene, from Portpatrick, Scotland, or Knockfergus, Ireland, *with passengers* to the West Indies in May 1656. [NA.SP25/77]

**HENDRY AND ANN OF MARYLAND,** master Samuel Wilson, arrived in Port Glasgow, Scotland, on 7 July 1690 from Virginia. [NAS.E72.15.18]

**HENRY,** master Christopher Moulthropp, from Limerick, Ireland, to Barbados and return in 1637. [NA.HCA.13/56/258, 491]

**HENRY AND FRANCIS OF NEWCASTLE,** 350 tons, master Richard Hutton, from Leith, via Montrose, Aberdeen, and Kirkwall, Scotland, *with passengers* bound for East New Jersey on 5 September 1685. [NAS.E72.15.32; RH18.1.93]

**HERCULES,** master Edward Say or Andrew Malloch, from Leith, Scotland, *with passengers* to Virginia in September 1673. [NAS.E72.15.17][RPCS.IV.83]

**HERMIN DE NANTES,** master Jean Dossett, from France to Martinique in 1701, captured by HMS Ruby and taken to Barbados. [SPAWI.1702/8]

**HET DRAATVAT,** master Jan Jansz Bestevaer, from Amsterdam, Holland, to the Nieuw Nederland in March 1657; from Nieuw Amsterdam in August 1657 bound for the Netherlands; from the Nieuw Nederland in August 1658 bound for the Netherlands. [CJR#46/55/106]

**HET EENDRACHT,** [The Concord], in the West Indies, 1651. [GAR.ONA.312.166.278]

**HET GEKRUYSTE HART,** [The Sacred Heart], master Dirck Jacobszoon Vries, from Holland on 20 January 1664 bound for the Nieuw Nederland, and arrived there on 17 April 1664; master Sievert Dircksz, returned from there in August 1664 to the Netherlands; from Amsterdam to the Nieuw Nederland, arrived there in February 1664, from Nieuw Amsterdam in May 1665 via

Bergen, Norway, to Holland. [CJR#342/346/358/378]
[NYCol.ms#14/83-123]

**HET GULDEN KOCK VAN VLISSINGEN,** [The Golden
Cock of Flushing], master Pieter Adriansen, from the
Netherlands *with passengers* to the Amazon in 1616,
similarly in 1618. [HS.2$^{nd}$ series, 171/164]

**HET HOFF VAN CLEEFF,** [The House of Cleves], master
Adriaen Bloomaert, from Amsterdam, Holland, *with
passengers* to the Nieuw Nederland in May 1652.
[NWI.I.122][GAA.NA#2279/iii/73]

**HET HUYS TE BUEREN,** [The Farmhouse], master Johan de
Vos, from Virginia to the Netherlands in 1650.
[GAR.ONA.135.324.437]

**HET LAM,** [The Lamb], master Pieter Corneliszoon De Huyt,
to the West Indies in 1608. [GAR.ONA.14.70.217]

**HET MARYAENS HOOFT,** master Pieter Revertsz., from
Virginia to Delftshaven, the Netherlands, in 1650.
[GAR.ONA.231.217.385]

**HET SWERTE HERDT,** from Amsterdam, Holland, to
Newfoundland in 1601. [GAA.NA90/4-5]

**HET TWEEDE HART,** [The Second Heart], in the West
Indies, 1638. [GAR.ONA.289.77.112]

**HET UTRECHT,** in the West Indies, 1630.
[GAR.ONA.303.205.210]

**HET VALGENDE,** from the Netherlands to Virginia in
November 1644. [GAR.ONA.96.53.78]

**HET VLIEGENDE HARP,** [The Flying Harp], master Jan
Aelwijnszoon, in the West Indies, 1636.
[GAR.ONA.302.187.356]

**HET VLIEGENDE HART VAN VLISSINGEN,** [The Flying
Heart of Flushing], arrived in Virginia on 15 December

1625 *with passengers,* and returned to the Low
Countries. [CSPCol.Vol.IV, 3.1.1626; 4.1627]

**HET VLIEGENDE HART,** [The Flying Heart], at Curacao in
1635; master Jan Alewijnszoon, at Pernambuco and St
Kitts in 1636 then to Delftshaven, the Netherlands; from
Pernambuco, St Kitts, and the West Indies, to the
Netherlands in 1637; from Rotterdam, Zealand, to St
Kitts in 1638. [NMM] [GAR.ONA.150.527.837/
85.421.836/ 293.81.101/86.70.132]

**HET VLIEGENDE HART,** [The Flying Heart], 300 tons,
from the Netherlands to Newfoundland in 1651.
[GAA.NA1574/262]

**HET VLIEGENDE HART,** [The Flying Heart], a galliot,
from Barbados and the West Indies to the Netherlands in
1669. [GAR.ONA.239.105.200/239.106.202]

**HET WAEKENDE HART,** in the West Indies, 1649.
[GAR.ONA.311.183.305]

**HET WAPEN VAN AMSTERDAM,** [The Arms of
Amsterdam], from the Nieuw Netherlands bound for the
Netherlands on 23 September 1626, arrived in
Amsterdam, Holland, on 4 November 1626; arrived in
Nieuw Amsterdam in 1628 from Africa. [VDV]
[DNY#1/37]

**HET WAPEN VAN DORDRECHT,** [The Arms of
Dordrecht], master Jacob Corneliszoon Van Oosthuysen,
from Helvoetssluys, the Netherlands, *with passengers*
bound via Africa, Pernambuco and St Kitts for the
Nieuw Nederland in 1640; master Jan Van Aller Az, at
Barbados, 1640. [GAR.ONA.86.197.357; 86.199.372]

**HET WAPEN DE FRANKRIJK,** [The Arms of France], a
Dutch prize, taken at Barbados in 1655.
[SPAWI.1655/1979]

**HET WAPEN VAN LEYDEN,** [The Arms of Leyden], master
Abraham Fernando Van Zeyle, at Ferryland,
Newfoundland, 1673. [NA.CO1.34.37/85]

**HET WAPEN VAN MEDEMBLICK,** [The Arms of
Medemblick], in the West Indies, 1646.
[GAR.ONA.334.145.361]

**HET WAPEN VAN NIEUW NEDERLAND,** [The Arms of
the Nieuw Nederland], to the Nieuw Nederland in 1646.
[GAA#817]

**HET WAPEN VAN NOORWEGEN,** [The Arms of Norway],
master Willem Claesen Ras, from Texel, Holland, *with
19 passengers* bound for Rensselaerwijk in the Nieuw
Nederland during May 1638, arrived in Nieuw
Amsterdam on 4 August 1638; from the Netherlands to
the Nieuw Nederland in 1639. [GAA]

**HET WAPEN VAN RENSSELAERWIJK,** [The Arms of
Rensselaerwijk], from Amsterdam, Holland, *with 16
passengers* bound for the Nieuw Nederland in September
1643, arrived in Nieuw Amsterdam during March 1644.
[NMM]

**HET WILDE HARDT,** [The Savage Heart], in the West
Indies, 1637. [GAR.ONA.293.79.99]

**HET WITTE LAM,** [The White Lamb], master Gerrit
Lambutsz, from Madeira to Rotterdam, Zealand, in 1643.
[GAR.ONA.263.530.475]

**HIRONDELLE,** [Swallow], from La Rochelle, France, *with
soldiers* to Canada in 1670. [BN.Melanges de Colbert
#176]

**HONORE DE LA ROCHELLE,** master Alain Durand, from
La Rochelle, France, to Quebec, the West Indies, and
return in 1670; to the West Indies in 1679; master
Francois Pillet, from La Rochelle to Quebec, the West
Indies, and return in 1681 and in 1682 under master
Pierre Gravoil; master Jacques Hurtin, from La Rochelle
to Quebec and back in 1683 and 1684; master Pierre
Soumande, to Quebec and the West Indies in 1685;
master Zacharie Aurillou, from La Rochelle to Quebec
and the West Indies in 1686 and 1687; master Abel

Ruelle from La Rochelle to Quebec in 1688; master
Jacques rasteau to Quebec *with passengers* in 1691 and
in 1692. [Charente Maritime Archives.B235/B5677/
B5678/B5680/B5682/B5687; Gironde Archives,
6B71/58; La Rochelle Library]

**HOPE OF COPENHAGEN,** when trading at St Kitts and
Nevis in 1654 was captured by the English and taken to
Plymouth, England, in 1655. [SPAWI.1655/39]
[Cal.SPCol.XII.422][NA.Inter-Regnum Entry Book,
Vol.CIII, 706, 725]

**HOPE OF DUBLIN,** a small pink, master Christopher
Tugwell, from Dublin, Ireland, bound for Jamaica in July
1667 when seized by the Fortune a French man o'war.
[Acts PCCol.#855][SPAWI.1699/1112]

**HOPE OF DUBLIN,** 150 tons, arrived in Dublin, Ireland,
from Barbados in October 1667; arrived in Galway,
Ireland, bound for Barbados in 1669.
[Cal.SPIre.1667/466; 1669/599]

**HOPE OF LEITH,** 350 tons, from Leith, Scotland, *with
passengers* bound for New York in October 1669, but
wrecked off Aberdeenshire, Scotland.
[NAS.GD29.106/1439/1962][RPCS.III.46][PCCol#841]
[ActsPCCol.1669/848][DNY#III/180]

**HOPE OF JERSEY,** 30 tons, from Jersey in the Channel
Islands bound for Jamaica and return via New England in
1672. [ActsPCCol.1673/957]

**HOPE OF EDINBURGH,** master Matthew Easton, from
Leith, Scotland, to New England in July 1681.
[NAS.E72.15.21/36]

**HOPE,** master James Millar, from Leith, Scotland, *with
passengers* to Darien on the Isthmus of Panama in 1698,
wrecked off Cuba on the return voyage.
[NAS.GD406.b.162, P40/13]

**HOPE OF BO'NESS,** master Richard Dalling, from Leith,
Scotland, to Darien in 1699. [NAS.GD406]

**HOPEFULL BINNING OF BO'NESS,** master Alexander Stark, from Leith, Scotland, to Darien on the Isthmus of Panama on 12 May 1699, arrived there in August 1699, from Darien *with passengers* to Jamaica in 1699. [OSN#22][NAS.GD406.1]

**HOPEWELL OF BOSTON,** master William Chichester, from Ireland via Antigua to Virginia in 1654. [Norfolk County Wills and Deeds, Vol. C, 159]

**HOPEWELL,** master Caleb Los, from Amsterdam, Holland, to New York in 1666. [NMM]

**HOPEWELL OF GALLOWAY,** to Barbados in 1666. [ActsPCCol.1668/744]

**HOPEWELL,** from Kinsale, Ireland, to Maryland in 1667. [ActsPCCol#765]

**HOPEWELL OF BRISTOL,** 200 tons, master Matthew Dean, from Antigua bound for Bristol, England, arrived in Kinsale, Ireland, and later in Cork, Ireland, in 1672. [ActsPCCol.1672/950]

**HOPEWELL OF BO'NESS,** from Port Glasgow, Scotland, bound for New York on 25 October 1672. [NAS.E72.19.6]

**HOPEWELL OF NEW YORK,** from Maryland via Dover bound for the Netherlands in 1682. [NA.E190/666/8]

**HOPEWELL OF BOSTON,** master James Duncan, arrived in Port Glasgow, Scotland, in July 1682 from Virginia; from Port Glasgow *with passengers* bound for New York in October 1682. [NAS.E72.19.5/6][RPCS.VII.534]

**HOPEWELL,** from the James River, Virginia, bound for Scotland in July 1695. [SPAWI.1695/329]

**HOPEWELL OF DUBLIN,** a 100 ton pink, master William Leggat, arrived in the Upper James River, Virginia, on

11 March 1699 *with 26 passengers* from Dublin via
Barbados; master James White, arrived in Virginia on 20
June 1700. [NA.CO5/1441]

IGNATIUS, from Bruges, Flanders, to the West Indies in
1667. [SPAWI.1667/1423]

INCREASE, master Phillip Popplestone, from Youghal,
County Cork, Ireland, *with 46 passengers* bound for
Maryland in 1679. [MSA.Patents#20/184]

INDIAN, from Amsterdam, Holland, to New York in 1667.

INDUSTRIE DE LA ROCHELLE, [The Industry of La
Rochelle], master Alain Du Rand, from La Rochelle,
France, to Quebec and the West Indies in 1694.
[Charente Maritime Archives.B5710][NAC]

INSULEN ST THOMAS, Captain Krillebasse, from Bergen,
Norway, to St Thomas in the Virgin Islands in October
1691. [RAK]

ISABEL OF BELFAST, master Richard Garner, arrived in
Port Glasgow, Scotland, from Barbados in October 1682.
[NAS.E72.19.5]

ISABELLA, 90 tons, via Ireland to the Leeward Islands in
1691. [ActsPCCol.20.8.1691]

IZAAC ET MARIE DE LA ROCHELLE, [Isaac and Mary
of La Rochelle], 120 tons, master Pierre Fougeron, from
La Rochelle, France, to Quebec and the West Indies in
1686. [Gironde Archives: 6B71/160; 6B291/131]

JACOB, [James], master David Jochemsen, from Amsterdam,
Holland, bound for New Orange in the Nieuw Nederland
in February 1674, arrived back in Amsterdam from the
Nieuw Nederland in October 1674. [DNY#2//735]

JAEGEREN, [Huntsman], from Copenhagen, Denmark, to St
Thomas, 1692; master Pieter Beck, from Brandenburg,
Germany, to St Thomas, Virgin Islands, in October 1693.
[DWI][RAK]

**JAMES OF AYR,** arrived in Ayr, Scotland, from Barbados in 1651. {see William Kelso's testament which was confirmed on 23 January 1651, and on 7 September 1652 with the Commissariat of Glasgow, NAS]

**JAMES OF BELFAST,** was impressed into Government service when in Antigua, and later, probably in 1667, was captured by the French off Guadaloupe; from Belfast, Ireland, via Glasgow, Scotland, in October 1670 *with passengers* bound for Montserrat and Nevis, arrived in Montserrat on 3 May 1671. Before September 1671 the ship was seized by the authorities in Nevis having broken the Navigation Acts.[ActsPCCol#755/1041] [NA.CO1.XXVIII/46][SPAWI.1671/631]

**JAMES OF LEITH,** 150 tons, from Leith, Scotland, *with passengers* to New York in 1669. [NAS,GD129/106] [ActsPCCol.1669/841,848-850]

**JAMES OF AYR,** 100 tons, master James Chambers, arrived in Ayr, Scotland, on 19 September 1673 from the West Indies; to the American Plantations *with passengers* in 1678; arrived in Ayr in 1678 from Montserrat; master John Harrison, from Ayr *with passengers* bound for the West Indies on 5 February 1681; arrived in Ayr on 19 September 1681 from the West Indies; from Ayr to the Caribee Islands on 13 March 1683; returned to Ayr on 7 September 1683 from Montserrat; master David Ferguson, from Ayr to Carolina on 19 August 1684. [NAS.E72.3.4/6/7/9/12/13][RPCS.V.528]

**JAMES OF LONDONDERRY,** 80 tons, master Thomas Browning, at Boston, New England, in June 1680. [SPAWI.1689/1374]

**JAMES OF WAIRWATER,** master John Stevenson, from Port Glasgow, Scotland, bound for the Caribee Islands on 15 February 1682. [NAS.E72.19.6]

**JAMES OF IRVINE,** master George Dredan, from Port Glasgow, Scotland, *with 4 passengers* bound for

Carolina in October 1682. [NAS.E72.19.6; NRAS. 0631/600]

**JAMES OF GLASGOW,** master William Anderson, from Glasgow, Scotland, to Virginia on 28 December 1685. [NAS.E72.19.12]

**JANE OF LONDON,** master Henry Stratford, from Barbados to Galway, Ireland, in May 1630. [NA.HCA.13/49/296]

**JANE OF BELFAST,** master Robert Murray, from Belfast, Ireland, to Virginia in 1692, but was captured off Newfoundland by a French privateer on the return voyage on 14 August 1692. [NA.HCA.Exams.Vol.80]

**JANE OF DUBLIN,** 100 tons, master William Thornton, sailed from Beaumaris, Wales, bound for Virginia, and was seized by the Collector of Potomac River, Virginia, on suspicion of smuggling, 1699, later in 1700 there was a trial before the Court of the Vice Admiralty of Virginia. [SPAWI.1700#234][ACV]

**JANE OF JERSEY,** master John D'Auvergne, from Boston, New England, to London in December 1699. [SPAWI.1699/1033]

**JANET OF LEITH,** master Robert Hay, from Leith, Scotland, to the West Indies in 1611. [NAS.E71.29.6/fo.22]

**JEAN OF LARGS,** master Ninian Gibson, from Port Glasgow, Scotland, bound for the West Indies in May 1684. [NAS.E72.19.9]

**JEAN OF LEITH,** from Scotland, lost off Greenland in 1686. [RPCS.XII.482]

**JEAN OF CHAILLEVETTE,** [The John of Chaillevette], 80 tons, master Jacques Thomas, from La Rochelle, France, to Quebec in 1691. [Charente Maritime Archives, B235]

**JEAN DE BORDEAUX,** [John of Bordeaux], master Pierre Rivier, arrived in Maryland by 1695; a French prize which was condemned in Annapolis, Maryland, on 5 July 1699. [DI.II.14][SPAWI.1699/597]

**JEAN CORNELIA,** from Havana, Cuba, bound for France, wrecked on Bermuda, 1702. [SPAWI.1702/1042]

**JEAN AND WILLIAM OF GLASGOW,** from Scotland to New England in 1678. [NAS.AC7.4]

**JEEMS,** at Curacao in 1645. [GAR.ONA.86.257.477]

**JEFRAU MARIA,** master Iver Hop, from Denmark to the West Indies in September 1687. [RAK]

**JERASMUS VAN ROTTERDAM,** master Francois de Bout, in the West Indies, 1634. [GAR.ONA.302.87.181]

**JEREMIAH OF BRISTOL,** 60 tons, master John Jonah, with a 10 man crew, from Bristol, England, via Kinsale, Ireland, to St John's, Newfoundland, in 1677. [NA.CO1/41, 168-170]

**JOB OF LEITH,** master John Gourlay, from Leith, Scotland, to Virginia, returned in March 1667. [NAS.E72.15.5]

**JOFFRAU CATARINA,** [The Virgin Catharine], master Jacob Dircksen Willree, from Amsterdam, Holland, via Guinea to Curacao, arrived there on 14 January 1665. [DI.I/167][NYCol.mss#17/104]

**JOHANNA OF GOSPORT,** a pink, from Ireland to Maryland, condemned by the Governor of Maryland in 1699. [SPAWI.1699/433]

**JOHN OF DUBLIN,** from Ireland to Avalon, Newfoundland, in 1662. [SPAWI.1662/386]

**JOHN OF SLIGO,** master Henry Jackson, from Sligo, Ireland, bound, via Spain, to the West Indies on 20 July 1669, but turned to piracy. [CSPIre]

**JOHN OF LONDON,** master Thomas Leider, from Leith, Scotland, to Virginia in January 1680; master James

Moodie, arrived in Glasgow, Scotland, on 27 October
1686 from the West Indies; master Daniel Pensax, from
Virginia via the Isle of Wight to Holland in 1689.
[NAS.AC7/5; E72.19.12][ActsPCCol.274/11]

**JOHN OF GLASGOW,** master John Hardy, from Port
Glasgow, Scotland, on 16 April 1681 bound for New
England; returned from there to Port Glasgow in
December 1681. [NAS.E72.19.1/2/5]

**JOHN OF LONDONDERRY,** master Andrew Cruickshank,
arrived in Port Glasgow, Scotland, on 17 September
1691 from Virginia. [NAS.E72.15.21]

**JOHN OF WEXFORD,** 60 tons, from Wexford, Ireland, to
the West Indies in 1690-1691. [ActsPCCol.1690/364, 26]

**JOHN AND DOROTHY OF LONDON,** master Thomas
Burley, from Virginia *with passengers* via Galway,
Ireland, to London, England, in 1635. [NA.HCA.13/52,
316]

**JOHN AND FRANCES,** possibly from Spain to Virginia in
1623. [RVC.IV.220]

**JOHN AND MARY,** master Samuel Morgan, with a crew of 6
men, from Limerick, Ireland, to Carbonear,
Newfoundland, in 1681. [NA.CO1/47, 113/121]

**JOHN AND NICHOLAS,** 180 tons, master Edward Barnes,
from Leith, Scotland, *with passengers* to the American
Plantations, (Barbados?), on 11 December 1685.
[RPCS.XI.386]

**JOHN AND THOMAS,** from Barbados via Alicante, Spain,
bound for Genoa, Italy, in 1640 (?) [NA.HCA.13/56/286]

**JOHN MEARNS,** arrived in Port Glasgow, Scotland, on 1
September 1696 from St Kitts. [NAS.E72.15.23]

**JOLLIE D'OLERON**, France, from the island of Savill
{Sable Island?}, Canada, in September 1627.
[NAS.AC7.1.109]

**JOLY,** [Pretty], Captain Beaujeau, from La Rochelle, France, on 24 July 1684 *with passengers* bound for the Mississippi, arrived in Haiti, Santa Domingo, in December 1684, from there bound for the Mississippi, later returned to France during 1686.[DCB.I..180] [BN.Collection Clairambault#1015/387; Collection Arnoul#21330]

**JONAS,** 100 tons, from La Rochelle, France, on 13 May 1606, *with passengers* bound for Port Royal, Acadia; arrived in New France in June 1607 from France; Captain Fleury or master Rene le Coq de la Saussaye, from Honfleur, France, *with passengers* on 12 March 1613 bound for Port Royal, Acadia, arrived there on 16 May 1613. [DCB.I.68/367/441/564]

**JONFRU GIERTRUD,** [The Lady Gertrude], master Frantz Weier, from Bergen, Norway, via Bordeaux, France, bound for St Thomas in the Virgin Islands in October 1691. [RAK]

**JONFRU MARGRETHE,** [The Lady Margaret], master Johannes Thors, from Gluckstad, Germany, via Guinea to St Thomas in July 1687. [RAK]

**JONGE BORNGARDT,** master Jacob Frantzen, from Brandenburg, Germany, to St Thomas, Virgin Islands, in March 1698. [RAK]

**JOSEPH,** from St Kitts *with passengers* bound for Waterford, Ireland, before 1640. [NA.HCA.13/55/419]

**JOSEPH OF BRISTOL,** arrived in Kinsale, Ireland, from Petuxan, Rhode Island, and Virginia on 16 April 1669. [Cal.SPIre.1666/1669.711]

**JOSEPH OF CORK,** 200 tons, master John Whiteing, from Cork, Ireland, bound for Virginia in 1691. [ActsPCCol.1691/364/55]

**JOSEPH AND DANIEL OF AYR,** master David Ferguson, from Ayr, Scotland, via Madeira to Maryland or Virginia in 1693. [NAS.B6.35.6]

**JUFFROUW ELYSABET,** [The Lady Elizabeth], master Heynrick Pieterszoon Halffhoren, from the Netherlands *with passengers* bound for Pernambuco and St Kitts in 1642. [GAR.ONA.86.269.505]

**JUFFROUW GEERTRUYD,** [The Lady Gertrude], master Dirck Lofreys, a Dutch vessel which was wrecked on the Bahamas on 17 March 1695. [SPAWI.1699/204]

**JUFFROUW LEONORA,** [The Lady Leonora], a 120 ton pinnace, from Amsterdam, Holland, *with passengers* to New York in 1668. [GAA#2845]

**JUSTICE,** Captain Guillet, from France on 24 May 1665 *with soldiers,* arrived in Quebec on 14 September 1665. [PAC]

**JUSTICE DE CALAIS,** [Justice of Calais], 100 tons, master Antoine Le Hot, from La Rochelle, France, to Quebec in 1687. [La Rochelle library, Groze#533][Charente Maritime Archives B5685]

**KALMAR NYCKEL,** [The Key of Kalmar], master Jan Hindricksen van der Water [or Peter Hollanders Ridder?], from Gothenburg, Sweden, via Medemblik, the Netherlands, and the West Indies *with passengers* to Nya Sverige, (New Sweden), in November 1637, arrived at Minquas Kill, Delaware, on 29 March 1638, returned to Sweden via St Kitts in 1638; master Cornelius van Vliet, from Gothenburg, Sweden, *with passengers* via Medemblik to Nya Sverige, (New Sweden), in 1638; master Pouwel Jamsen, from Texel, Holland, *with passengers* bound for Nya Sverige, (New Sweden), on 7 February 1640, lande at Fort Christina, there, on 17 April 1640; master Adrian Jansen, from Sweden *with Swedish and Finnish passengers* bound for Nya Sverige, (New Sweden), in 1641; from Gothenburg via the West Indies to Nya Sverige, (New Sweden), in 1643, arrived there on

12 March 1644. [SD#30-33][HDC.ii.2][DNY#1/291]
[SSD#758] [PMHB.III.462]

**KATHERINE,** possibly from Ireland to Barbados in 1653.
[see BA:rb6/13/30]

**KATHERINE OF LONDON,** master John Lakey, from
Glasgow, Scotland, to Virginia on 29 December 1685.
[NAS.E72.19.12]

**KATHERINE OF GLASGOW,** master James Wilson, arrived
in Glasgow on 10 September 1686 from Virginia.
[NAS.E72.19.12]

**KOBENHAVN BORS,** [Copenhagen Exchange], master Innes
Pieters, from Denmark via Guinea to St Thomas, Virgin
Islands, in September 1698. [DWI]

**L'AIGLE,** [The Eagle], from France to Martinique in 1695.
[ISE.323]

**L'AIGLE D'OR DE BROAGE,** [The Golden Eagle of
Broage], 300 tons, master Nicolas Gargot de La Broage,
from France to Canada in July 1662 *with soldiers and
indentured servants*, arrived at Grand Placentia,
Newfoundland, in October 1662, then to Tadousac,
Quebec, on 27 October 1662, from there on 20
November 1662, arrived in France in January 1663, to
Canada *with indentured servants* in 1663, arrived in
Quebec on 22 September 1663; from La Rochelle *with
200 soldiers* bound for Quebec on 13 May 1665, landed
on 18 August 1665; from La Rochelle to Canada in 1666.
[Savin, La Rochelle; Moreau, La Rochelle, La Rochelle
library] [BN.Melanges de Colbert#109/136][DCB.1.296,
602] [NAC]

**L'AIGLE DE BORDEAUX,** [The Eagle of Bordeaux], 120
tons, master Elie Grassen, to Quebec in 1698, from
Quebec on 31 October 1698, wrecked during November
1698. [Archives Departmentales de la Gironde,
6B/298/30.5.1698]

**L'AIGLE NOIR DE LA ROCHELLE,** [The Black Eagle of La Rochelle], 150 tons, master P. Gentet, from La Rochelle, France, to Quebec in 1676; to Quebec and the West Indies in 1677; master Jean Chauvet, to Quebec and the West Indies in 1678; under master Jacques Pruneau to Quebec and the West Indies in 1679; to Canada in 1683; from La Rochelle to Canada and the West Indies in 1685. [La Rochelle Municipal Library ms]

**L'AIMABLE,** [Kind], a 180 ton flute, master Claude Aygron, from La Rochelle, France, on 24 July 1684 *with passengers* bound for the Mississippi, arrived in Haiti in December 1684, from there bound for the Mississippi but wrecked in Matagordo Bay in 1686. [DCB.I.180] [La Rochelle Municipal Library ms][Charente Maritime Archives ms]

**L'AIMABLE DE LA ROCHELLE,** [The Friendly of La Rochelle], 80 tons, master Jean Germon, from La Rochelle, France, to Canada in 1691. [Charente Maritime Archives ms]

**L'AIMABLE,** from Brest, France, to Placentia, Newfoundland in August 1692. [ISE.347]

**L'AMITIE,** [The Friendship], a sloop, master Jens Hendrichsen, from Copenhagen, Denmark, to Hudson Bay on 9 May 1619, arrived there on 7 September 1619, from there on 26 June 1620 bound for Norway, arrived there on 21 September 1620. [DCB.I.515]

**L'AMITIE DE LA ROCHELLE,** [The Friendship of La Rochelle], 80 tons, from France *with 8 passengers* bound for Acadia on 26 March 1649; master Francois Flandreau, from La Rochelle, France, to Quebec in 1686. [Charente Maritime archives ms]

**L'AMITIE,** [The Friendship], a 150 ton frigate, master Nicolas Gratton, arrived in Quebec during 1666. [NAC]

**L'ANGE BLANC,** [The White Angel], 80 tons, master Elie Raymond, arrived in Quebec in 1662. [NAC]

**L'ANGE BLANC DE FLESSINGUE,** [The White Angel of Flushing], 200 tons, master Andre Chaviteau, arrived in Quebec *with indentured servants* on 29 June 1664. [NAC]

**L'ANGE BLANC DE QUEBEC,** [The White Angel of Quebec], 300 tons, master Andrew Chavitant, arrived in Quebec in 1666. [NAC]

**L'ANGE GABRIEL,** [The Angel Gabriel], arrived in Quebec in August 1647. [NAC]

**L'ANGE ST MICHEL,** [St Michael the Angel], at Port Royal, Acadia, 1616. [DCB.1.476]

**L'ANGLOIS,** [The Englishman], arrived in Quebec in August 1649. [NAC]

**L'ARC EN CIEL,** [The Rainbow], at Placentia, Newfoundland, in August 1687. [B.N.Colln.Arnoul#21334]

**L'ARCHANGE SAINT MICHEL DE AMSTERDAM,** [The Archangel Michael of Amsterdam], 130 tons, master Louis Maheut, from France to Acadia in 1680. [La Rochelle Municipal Library ms]

**L'ARMES D'AMSTERDAM,** [The Arms of Amsterdam], 250 tons, master Jean Guillonneau, from La Rochelle, France, to Quebec in 1657; master Jacob Gilles, arrived in Quebec on 20 August 1657. [La Rochelle Municipal Library][NAC]

**L'ARMES D'ANGLETERRE,** [The Arms of England], master Joseph-Antoine Le Febre de la Barre, in the West Indies, 1667. [DCB.I.443]

**L'ARMES DE FRANCE,** [The Arms of France], 170 tons, master Elie Abrard, from la Rochelle, France, to Canada and the West Indies in 1684. [Charente Maritime Archives]

**L'ARMES DE LA COMPAGNIE DE LA ROCHELLE,**
[The Arms of the Company of La Rochelle], 100 tons,
master P. D. de Bonaventure, from La Rochelle, France,
to Canada in 1690, under master N. Robbillard in 1691,
and under master Charles Francois in 1692. [Charente
Maritime archives]

**L'ARMES DE ZELANDE,** [The Arms of Zealand], 250 tons,
master Janner de Combes, from La Rochelle, France, to
Quebec and Newfoundland in 1662, landed at Quebec on
4 July 1662. [La Rochelle Municipal Library][NAC]

**L'ASSIERE,** Captain Delligree, at Martinique, 1702.
[SPAWI.1702/195]

**L'AVENANT,** [The Pleasing], arrived in Acadia on 16
September 1699 from France. [ASC#120]

**L'ELIE DE MARENNES,** from La Rochelle, France, to
Acadia in 1621.

**L'EMBUSCADE,** master M. de la Caffiniere, from La
Rochelle, France, on 31 July 1689 bound for
Chedabucto, arrived there on 13 September 1689; from
Port Royal, Acadia, on 8 November 1689 bound for
France, arrived at Rochefort on 23 December 1689.
[ASC#192]

**L'EMERILLON,** from France to the West Indies in 1691.
[ISE.315]

**L'ENVIEUX,** from France to Canada in 1692; from France to
the West Indies in 1694, returned to La Rochelle in
December 1694. [ISE.316/318/339]

**L'EOLE,** from France to the West Indies in 1690. [ISE.308]

**L'ESPERANCE,** from La Rochelle, France, to the West Indies
in March 1696, [ISE.322]; Captain de Legollissomiere,
at Martinique, 1702. [SPAWI.1702/195]

**L'ESPRIT DU BOIS D'OLONNE,** [The Wood Spirit of
Olonne], master Peter Giraudeau, from Newfoundland to

France, when captured by the English and taken to Plymouth in July 1676. [ActsPCCol.1676/1105]

**L'HYRONDELLE,** from Boston, New England, to La Rochelle, France, in December 1685. [Mass. Arch. French Docs. Vol.3]

**L'IMPERTINENT,** from France to Quebec in 1693. [ISE.339]

**L'INCOGNUE,** from La Rochelle, France, to the West Indies in April 1696. [ISE.322]

**L'INFANTE DE LA ROCHELLE,** [The Child of La Rochelle], Captain Vergnian, was captured off Acadia by Dutch vessels in 1677. [Charente Maritime Archives, 26.10.1677]

**L'INTREPIDE,** from La Rochelle, France, to the West Indies in April 1696. [ISE.322]

**L'INVINCIBLE,** Captain Le Ceguillo, at Martinique, 1702. [SPAWI.1702/195]

**L'ORRIFLAME,** Captain de Pasle, at Martinique, 1702. [SPAWI.1702/195]

**LA BADINE,** from France to the West Indies and return in 1694-1695, and in 1695. [ISE.312/324]

**LA BOUFFONNE,** from France to Quebec in 1694. [ISE.340]

**LA BRAVE DE LA ROCHELLE,** from La Rochelle, France, to Bicq, near Tadoussac on the St Lawrence River in 1620.

**LA BRETONNE,** from France *with passengers* to Canada in 1694. [DCB.1.427]

**LA BRETONNE,** from France to Acadia in August 1693. [ISE.340]

**LA CHARENTE,** from France to Quebec in August 1693; and in 1694. [ISE.340]

**LA FLEUR DE MAI,** from Quebec on 16 November 1690
bound for La Rochelle, arrived there on 12 January 1691;
from France on 28 July 1691 bound for Quebec, arrived
there on 18 September 1691. [OC#15]

**LA FRIPONNE,** from France to Port Royal, Acadia, in 1688;
from France to the West Indies in April 1689.
[ASC#174][ISE.304]

**LA GAILLARDE,** at Port Royal in 1698. [ASC#186]

**LA GEROON,** a French privateer at St Kitts in 1629. [HS.2$^{nd}$
series, 56/19]

**LA JARDIN DE HOLLANDE,** Captain Jean Guillon, from
France to Plaisance, Newfoundland, in 1663.
[DCB.I.296]

**LA LEVRETTE DE HAVRE DE GRACE,** master Jean
Rossignol, from Le Havre, France, to Canada and return
in 1603-1604. [WSC]

**LA LOIRE,** from La Rochelle, France, to the West Indies in
1695. [ISE.324]

**LA MADELEINE,** a barque, from La Rochelle to Mentane on
the St Lawrence River in 1614. [RB#49][TD#167]

**LA MARIE DE SAINT JEAN DE LUZ,** from La Rochelle,
France, in 1599 bound for North America. [BD#336]

**LA NOTRE DAME D'ESPERANCE,** from Ciboure near
Saint Jean de Luz, France, to Gaspe, Canada, in 1599.
[BD#336]

**LA PAIX,** [The Peace], 300 tons, master Elie Siberon, from
La Rochelle, France, *with indentured servants* bound
for Quebec in 1664; master Ethier Guillon, from La
Rochelle *with soldiers* bound for Quebec in 1665,
arrived there on 18 August 1664. ]Charente Maritime
Archives, b5665][DCB.I.602]

LA PAIX, [The Peace], a French pirate vessel which was captured and taken to Hampton, Virginia, in 1700. [SPAWI.1700/523x-xiv]

LA PELICAN DE ST MALO, [The Pelican of St Malo], master Nicholas Le Breton, from Montserrat to Galway, Ireland, in 1649. [NA.COI.XII.25][SPAWI.1654/25]

LA PELICAN, [The Pelican], from La Rochelle, France, to Placentia, Newfoundland, in 1696, sunk in battle in Hudson Bay during September 1697. [BN.Collection. Clairmabault.277/153]

LA PERLE, [The Pearl], from France to Martinique in March 1689; from La Rochelle, France, *with passengers* to Quebec in 1693; master Charles Chaviteau, from La Rochelle to Quebec in 1696; master Jean Paradis, from La Rochelle to Quebec and the West Indies in 1698, 1699, and 1700. [ISE.304][Charente Maritime Archives, B5691-B5696]

LA PERROQUOT DE LA ROCHELLE, [The Parrot of La Rochelle], master Pierre Monbeuil, from La Rochelle, France, to Acadia and Quebec in 1680. [Charente Maritime Archives, B5679; Teuleron ms]

LA PETITE NOTRE DAME DU HAVRE, [The Little Our Lady of Le Havre], 100 tons, from France *with passengers* bound for Martinique on 26 August 1635. [PRM#11]

LA PETITE SUZON DE LA ROCHELLE, [The Little Susan of La Rochelle], 60 tons, master Jean Guillet, from Bordeaux, France, to Quebec in 1683. [Gironde Archives, 6B289]

LA PLUME DE LA ROCHELLE, [The Golden Pen of La Rochelle], 170 tons, master Jean Goislin, from Nantes, France, to Quebec on 13 July 1671; master Jean Grignon, from France to Quebec in 1672 but captured by the Dutch. [WMQ.LII.96][La Rochelle Archives, Teuleron #83, Ferrand; Charente Maritime Archives B5672]

**LA PLUME D'OR,** [The Golden Feather], from France to Quebec in 1672, lost at sea. [BN.Melanges de Colbert #161]

**LA ROCHELAISE DE LA ROCHELLE,** 300 tons, master Pierre Gentet, from La Rochelle, France, to Plaisance, Newfoundland, in 1680. [Charente Maritime Archives, B5679]

**LA ROYALE,** [The Royal], 60 tons, Captain Herbouin, from St Kitts on 6 May 1681, arrived in France on 15 September 1681. [SPAWI.1681/236]

**LA ROYALE PAIX,** [The Royal Peace], from La Rochelle, France, on 20 August 1699 *with passengers* bound for Acadia, arrived at Port Royale on 13 October 1699. [ASC#176]

**LA VESTE,** [The Jacket], master .... La Grange, from La Rochelle, France, to Quebec in 1696. [La Rochelle Archives, Gariteau]

**LA VIERGE DE LA ROCHELLE,** [The Virgin of La Rochelle], 320 tons, at the St John River, 1642; 120 tons, master H. Bourget, arrived in Quebec in June 1644; master Pierre Boileau, arrived in Quebec on 13 October 1651; master Fabien Marot, from La Rochelle, France, arrived in Quebec on 27 May 1657. [DCB.1.504][NAC] [La Rochelle Archives, Savin][Charente Maritime archives, Teuleron]

**LA VIERGE DE LA ROCHELLE,** [The Virgin of La Rochelle]. 350 tons, master Michel Detcheverry, from La Rochelle, France, to Newfoundland, in 1677; master Pierre Catalogne, from La Rochelle to Newfoundland in 1679. [La Rochelle Archives, Teuleron#50]

**LA VILLE DE BAYONNE,** [The Town of Bayonne], from La Rochelle, France, to Placentia, Newfoundland, in 1696. [BN.Collection Clairmabault, 277/153]

**LA VILLE DE BORDEAUX,** [The Town of Bordeaux], from Bordeaux, France, to Canada in 1692.[NAC]

**LA VILLE DE LISBONNE DE LA ROCHELLE,** [The Town of Lisbon of La Rochelle], 120 tons, master Pierre Durand, from La Rochelle, France, to Quebec and the West Indies in 1684. [Charente Maritime Archives, B5682]

**LA VILLE DE ROUEN,** [The Town of Rouen], from France to Canada in 1670. [BN.Melanges de Colbert#176]

**LA VILLE MARIE DE LA ROCHELLE,** master Jean Couillandeau, from La Rochelle, France, to Quebec and the West Indies in 1695, also in 1697, and in 1699. [La Rochelle Archives, Gariteau; Gironde Archives 6B77/247; Charente Maritime Archives, B235/338, B5691, B5694, and B5695]

**LAMB OF AYR,** from Ayr, Scotland, possibly via Belfast, Ireland, to Barbados in 1673. [NAS.B6.24.3]

**LAUREL OF WHITEHAVEN,** master Peter Languine, from Virginia to Rotterdam, Zealand, in 1685. [NAS.Russell.ms#858]

**LE BIGUARE,** Captain Villar, at Martinique, 1702. [SPAWI.1702/195]

**LE BIZARRE,** from France to the West Indies in 1690. [ISE.308]

**LE BON,** from Brest, France, to Placentia, Newfoundland, in August 1692, returned from Placenta on 20 November 1692; from La Rochelle, France, to the West Indies in 1695. [ISE.324, 347]

**LE BOURBON,** from La Rochelle, France, to the West Indies in 1695. [ISE.324]; Captain Le Conte de Blanac, at Martinique, 1702. [SPAWI.1702/195]

**LE CALLAISIEN,** from France to Canada in 1673. [BN.864/fos.25-51]

**LE CAPABLE,** Captain De La Roize, at Martinique, 1702.
[SPAWI.1702/195]

**LE CHASSEUR D'AMSTERDAM,** [The Hunter], 120 tons,
Captain Terrier, arrived in Quebec on 14 July 1650.
[NAC][Charente Maritime archives, Moreau]

**LE CHEVAL MARIN,** from France to the West Indies, 1691;
from France to Martinique in 1695. [ISE.308/315/323]

**LE COMTE DE TOULOUSE,** from France to Mexico and
return in 1694. [ISE.326]

**LE CONCORDE,** was captured and taken to Barbados in
1701. [SPAWI.1702/1012]

**LE CONSTANT,** Captain Le Manchan, at Martinique, 1702.
[SPAWI.1702/195]

**LE COROSSOL,** from France to Quebec in 1693. [ISE.339]

**LE DAUPHIN DE DIEPPE,** from France to New France in
1620.

**LE DAUPHIN,** Captain Du Pissencour, at Martinique, 1702.
[SPAWI.1702/195]

**LE DESIRE,** from La Rochelle, France, to New France on 3
February 1624.

**LE DON DE DIEU DE MARENNES,** from La Rochelle,
France, bound for Acadia on 21 March 1623, returned to
La Rochelle in September 1623.

**LE FAUCON,** from France to the West Indies in 1694.
[ISE.311]

**LE FAVORI,** from France to Martinique in 1695. [ISE.323]

**LE FIRM,** Captain du Pallay, at Martinique, 1702.
[SPAWI.1702/195]

**LE FORT,** Captain Le de Parron Depelliere, at Martinique, 1702. [SPAWI.1702/195]

**LE FORTUNE,** from La Rochelle, France, to New France on 3 February 1624.

**LE FRANCOIS,** from France to the West Indies in 1690. [ISE.308]

**LE GAILLARD,** from Bayonne, France, to Newfoundland in 1694; from La Rochelle, France, to the West Indies in April 1696. [ISE.322, 349]

**LE GRAND ARMAND,** 250 tons, from Nantes, France, to Martinique in 1646, and return via Ireland and England in 1647. [TA#121]

**LE GRAND ST JOSEPHE DE LA ROCHELLE,** [The Great St Joseph of La Rochelle], master Jean Grignon, from Bordeaux, France, to Canada in March 1676; master Jean Grignon, from Bordeaux to Canada in April 1677; master Francois Dalton, from Bordeaux to Canada in 1680. [Gironde Archives, 6B67/9; Charente Maritime Archives, B5677/8; La Rochelle Archives, Teuleron]

**LE HAZARDEUX,** from France to the West Indies in 1694; master le Sieur du Tast, from France bound for Quebec, arrived there on 12 July 1691. [ISE.316, 339]

**LE HENRY,** Captain de Condray, at Martinique, 1702. [SPAWI.1702/195]

**LE JARDIN DE HOLLANDE,** [The Garden of Holland], 300 tons, master Jean Guillon de Laubatiel, from La Rochelle, France, on 3 June 1663, bound for Plaisance, Newfoundland, and Quebec, arrived in Quebec on 22 September 1663; from Quebec on 26 October 1663 bound for France; master .... De Bouiges, from La Rochelle *with passengers* on 22 June 1665, arrived in Quebec on 14 September 1665; from Quebec on 14 October 1665 and arrived in France on 1 December 1665. [Charente Maritime Archives.B5665][DCB.I.296]

**LE JEAN DE LA ROCHELLE,** master Daniel Braignault, from La Rochelle, France, to Mentane on the St Lawrence River in 1616. [BD#350]

**LE JEAN DE MORTAGNE,** from La Rochelle, France, to Acadia in 1621.

**LE JEHAN,** from La Rochelle, France, to Canada in 1621.

**LE JONAS DE HONFLEUR,** from La Rochelle *with passengers* bound for New France in 1606. [BD#336-340]

**LE JOSEPH,** from La Rochelle, France, to Quebec in 1651(?). [Charente Maritime archives, Savin/Teuleron]

**LE JUSTE,** Captain Carouch Allart, at Martinique, 1702. [SPAWI.1702/195]

**LE MERVEILLEUX,** master Vice Admiral Chateau Renaud, at Martinique, 1702. [SPAWI.1702/195]

**LE MIGNON,** from France to the West Indies in April 1689. [ISE.304]

**LE MODERE,** Captain Bombron, at Martinique, 1702. [SPAWI.1702/195]

**LE MONARCH,** master Le Marquis Nerman, at Martinique, 1702. [SPAWI.1702/195]

**LE NEPTUNE,** from France to the West Indies in 1690. [ISE.308]

**LE NICOLAS DE ST GILLES,** 100 tons, master Henri Langevin, from La Rochelle, France, to Acadia in 1636.[Charente Maritime archives, Teuleron, charter

**LE NOIR,** [The Black], from France *with 51 passengers* to Canada in 1664. [Charente Maritime Archives, B5665/10]

**LE OLE,** Captain de Ferrerie, at Martinique, 1702.
[SPAWI.1702/195]

**LE ORGELEUX,** Captain Le Chevalier de Chateau Regnant,
at Martinique, 1702. [SPAWI.1702/195]

**LE PELICAN,** from Bayonne, France, to Newfoundland in
1694. [ISE.349]

**LE PESSELANT,** Captain de Serbie, at Martinique, 1702.
[SPAWI.1702/195]

**LE PETIT FRANCOIS,** [The Little Francis], 50 tons, master
P. De La Ford, was captured at sea by the Spanish when
bound for Quebec in 1655. [NAC]

**LE PETIT SAINT CHRISTOPHE,** [The Little St
Christopher], 50 tons, master I. Richard, arrived in
Quebec in September 1646. [NAC]

**LE PETIT SAINT JEAN,** [The Little St John], master J.
Coupereau, arrived in Quebec during November 1638;
master Rene Boutin, arrived in Quebec on 18 August
1651; arrived in Quebec in 1652; arrived in Quebec
during 1652. [NAC]

**LE PETIT SAINT JEAN DU CANADA,** [The Little St John
of Canada], arrived in Canada during 1673. [NAC]

**LE PETIT SAINT LUC DE BROAGE,** from La Rochelle,
France, to Acadia in 1634. [Charente Maritime archives,
Juppin]

**LE PHOENIX,** from La Rochelle, France, to the West Indies
in April 1696. [ISE.322]

**LE PLAISIR,** from La Rochelle, France, on 5 March 1620,
bound for Acadia, returned to La Rochelle in September
1620.

**LE PLAISIR DE LA ROCHELLE,** [The Pleasure of La
Rochelle], master Jean Guilloneau, from La Rochelle,
France, to Acadia in 1661; master Pierre Thomas, from

La Rochelle to Acadia in 1664. [La Rochelle Archives, Moreau#27]

**LE POLI,** from France to Quebec in 1692; master Pierre Le Moyne d'Iberville, arrived in Quebec in 1693. [ISE#339][ASC#180][NAC]

**LE PONT CHARTRAIN DE LA ROCHELLE,** master Jean Javeleau, from Bordeaux, France, to Quebec in 1692; from France to Quebec and Newfoundland in 1693; from France to Quebec in 1694; master Jean Couillandeau, from La Rochelle, France, to Quebec and the West Indies in 1695; master Jean Javeleau, from La Rochelle, France, to the West Indies, Newfoundland and Canada in April 1696; from France to Quebec and the West Indies in 1699. [ISE.322][Gironde Archives, 6B75/87.78.1-64, 6B296, 6B298; Charente Maritime Archives.B5691/2]

**LE POSTILLION,** from La Rochelle, France, to Canada in 1613. [RB#50]

**LE POSTILLON DE LA ROCHELLE,** [The Coach of La Rochelle], 100 tons, master Pierre Thomas, from La Rochelle, France, to Quebec and the West Indies in 1673; from France to Quebec in 1693. [Charente Maritime Archives B5672/3][La Rochelle Archives, Riviere & Soulard]

**LE PROFOND,** [The Thorough], master .... Bonaventure, from Rochefort, France, bound for Quebec, Acadia and Newfoundland, in July 1696. [BN][FCA.ACClld.3/170]

**LE PROPHETE ELIE DE LA ROCHELLE,** [The Prophet Elias of La Rochelle], from La Rochelle, France, to Quebec in 1667. [La Rochelle Archives, Teuleron#101]

**LE PRUDENT,** Captain de Grandpre, at Martinique, 1702. [SPAWI.1702/195]

**LE RENAU,** from La Rochelle, France, to the West Indies in April 1696, from there via Placentia, Newfoundland, to France. [ISE.322]

**LE ROUE DE FORTUNE,** [The Wheel of Fortune], master Isaac Gabiou, from La Rochelle, France, to Quebec and Newfoundland in May 1695. [Charente Maritime Archives B5691; La Rochelle Archives, Gariteau ms]

**LE SACRIFICE D'ABRAHAM,** [The Sacrifice of Abraham], 300 tons, master Elie Raymond, arrived in Quebec in 1658; master Isie Guyesmeax, arrived in Quebec in 1659; master Jean Monbeauil, from La Rochelle, France, to New England in 1674; master Jean Monbeuil, from La Rochelle to Newfoundland in 1675 and in 1676. [NAC] [Charente Maritime Archives, 21.4.1674; # B5674/5] [La RochelleArchives, Vigneros. NEQ.13.99]

**LE SAGE DE BORDEAUX,** [The Wise Man of Bordeaux], master Phillipe Sage, from France to Quebec in 1689; from Bordeaux, France, to Quebec and the West Indies in 1691. [Bordeaux Archives, Loste ms 251; Gironde Archives 6B75/17, 6B295/220]

**LE SAINT ANDRE,** [The St Andrew], from La Rochelle, France, *with107 passengers* bound for Quebec in 1659. [FH.7.396]

**LE SAINT FRANCOIS,** from La Rochelle, France, to Acadia in 1640. [FH.7.310]

**LE SAINT GEORGES,** from La Rochelle, France, to Canada in 1599. [TD#136, 165]

**LE SAINT JEAN,** master Andre Camus, from La Rochelle, France, *with 30 passengers* bound for Acadia in Spring 1640. [Charente Maritime archives, Teuleron, fo.3]

**LE SAINT JOSEPH,** from La Rochelle, France, to Miscou on the Gaspe coast in 1646, returning to La Rochelle in November 1646. [Charente Maritime archives, Teuleron]

**LE SAINT LOUIS DE LES SABLES D'OLONNE,** from France to New France in 1620.

**LE SAINT LOUIS,** Captain de Genisne Mounier, at Martinique, 1702. [SPAWI.1702/195]

**LE SAINT LUC,** from La Rochelle, France, bound for Canada in 1621.

**LE SALAMANDRE,** [The Salamander], from France to Tadoussac on the St Lawrence River in 1621. [BNF#131]

**LE SOLEIL,** from France bound for Mentane on the St Lawrence River in March 1614, but shipwrecked near Tadoussac.[RB#49][TD#167]

**LE SOLEIL D'AFRIQUE DE ROCHEFORT,** [The African Sun of Rochefort], master … Delorme, from Rochefort, France, to Canada and Hudso's Bay in 1688; master Simon Pierre de Bonaventure, from La Rochelle bound for Quebec and Acadia in 1691, arrived in Quebec on 1 July 1691. [DCB.I.577][Charente Maritime Archives, B235][La Rochelle Archives, Riviers & Soulard] [ISE.339][ASC#164]

**LE SOLEIL COURONNE DE LA ROCHELLE,** [The Crowned Sun of La Rochelle]. 200 tons, master Pierre Gaigneur, from Bordeaux, France, to Quebec and the West Indies in 1680. [Gironde Archives, 6B68/16]

**LE SOLIDE,** from France to the West Indies 1691. [ISE.315]; Captain Chambellin, at Martinique, 1702. [SPAWI.1702/195]

**LE SUPERBE,** Captain Chareloyre, at Martinique, 1702. [SPAWI.1702/195]

**LE SURRENE,** Captain de Mongron, at Martinique, 1702. [SPAWI.1702/195]

**LE TEMERAIRE,** from Brest, France, to Placentia, Newfoundland, in August 1692; from France to the West Indies in 1694. [ISE.316/347]

**LE TRYDENT,** Captain Devaine, at Martinique, 1702. [SPAWI.1702/195]

**LE VAILLANT,** from France to the West Indies in 1690. [ISE.308]

**LE VAINQUEUR DE LA ROCHELLE,** [The Victor of La Rochelle], 120 tons, master Yves Marot, from La Rochelle, France, to Quebec and the West Indies in 1697. [Charente Maritime Archives, B5693]

**LE VERIE DE NANTES,** arrived in Quebec in 1654. [NAC]

**LE VERMANDOIS,** from France to the West Indies in 1690. [ISE#307]

**LE VINGEUR,** Captain Rose Maonq, at Martinique, 1702. [SPAWI.1702/195]

**LE VOLLANTIERE,** Captain Lanquin, at Martinique, 1702. [SPAWI.1702/195]

**LEVRETTE,** from France to Canada in 1608. [DCB.I.208]

**LE WESP,** from France to the West Indies and return in 1694-1695. [ISE.312]

**LIVER OF LIVERPOOL,** 130 tons, master James Kilner, arrived in the Delaware River in July 1683 from Dublin.

**LOUIS MARIE DE LA ROCHELLE,** master Thomas Fleurisson, from France to Quebec in 1688. [La Rochelle Library, Berthellot pp; Gironde Archives, 6B72/153, 6B294/19; 6B1056]

**LOUIS DE LA ROCHELLE,** [Louis of La Rochelle], master Michel Cande, from Bordeaux, France, to Quebec and the West Indies in May 1689. [Charente Maritime Archives, B235/193; Gironde Archives, 6B73/132]

**LOVE OF LONDON,** from Barbados to Scotland on 2 July 1658. [NAS.NRAS.0361/box 24]

**LOVEN,** [The Lion], from Denmark to Greenland in 1605; master John Cunningham, from Denmark to Labrador in 1606. [DCB.I.243]

**LOVEN,** master Willem Adrianssen, from Brandenburg, Germany, to St Thomas, Virgin Islands, in March 1692. [RAK]

**LOYALTY OF BELFAST,** 1 60 ton pink, master Robert Murray, arrived in the Rappahannock River, Virginia, in 1699. [NA.CO5/1441]

**LUCRETIA,** from Jamaica to Cork in 1705. [CalSPDom.SP63/365/127]

**LYON OF DIEPPE,** a pinnace, master William de Caen, from Quebec to France in 1633. [SPAWI.1633/75]

**MADAME THORMOHLEN,** from Denmark to St Thomas in the Virgin Islands in November 1691; from Copenhagen to St Thomas in 1692. [RAK][DWI]

**MADELEINE,** 80 tons, master J. Jouet, arrived in Quebec in August 1643. [NAC]

**MAERTEN VAN ROFFEN VAN MIDDELBURG,** [Martin van Roffen of Middleburg], 350 tons, master Leonard Johnson, in the West Indies during 1662. [SPAWI.1662/253]

**MAGDALEINE,** from Dieppe, France, *with passengers* bound for Canada on 28 April 1628. [DCB.I.579]

**MARCHANDS ADVENTURE,** from Ireland to Barbados in 1668. [SPAWI.1699/1112]

**MARECHAL DE LA ROCHELLE,** [The Blacksmith of La Rochelle], master Jean Guillot, from La Rochelle, France, to Quebec and the West Indies in 1688. [BN#ms.11335/194]

**MAREKATTEN,** [Sea Cat], from Denmark to Greenland in 1603. [DCB.I/243]

**MARGARET OF LEITH,** 178 tons, master Edward Burd, from Leith, Scotland, *with passengers* to Barbados in

1666; from Barbados bound for Scotland but impressed into government service and later lost in a hurricane in 1667. [RPCS.II/642][NAS.HH1.11][SPAWI.1667/1523] [ActsPCCol.1668/748]

**MARGARET OF MORFIN,** master William Glover, from Port Glasgow, Scotland, to Virginia in April 1684. [NAS.E72.19.9]

**MARGARET OF NEW YORK,** master James Duncan, from Holland bound for New York in 1692. [ActsPCCol.1692/467, 4]

**MARGARET OF DUNDEE,** master Leonard Robertson, from Dundee, Scotland, to Darien on the Isthmus of Panama in March 1700. [NAS.GD406]

**MARGRIET VAN ALBANY,** [Margaret of Albany], master David Eduwarts, from New York to Amsterdam in September 1670; from Amsterdam to New York in 1671. [CJR#426]

**MARGUERITE,** [Margaret], 70 tons, arrived in Quebec in August 1647. [NAC]

**MARGUERITE DE BROUAGE,** [Margaret of Brouage], 300 tons, master Guillaume Hurtin, from France to Acadia in 1661. [La Rochelle library, Moreau #64]

**MARGUERITE DE LA ROCHELLE,** [Margaret of La Rochelle], master Guillaume Huertin, arrived in Quebec in 1661; master Jean Des Bois, from France to Acadia in 1664. [NAC][Charente Maritime Archives #B5615]

**MARGUERITE DE DIEPPE,** [Margaret of Dieppe], 45 tons, master David Chretien, from La Rochelle, France, to Canada and the West Indies in 1686. [La Rochelle Library, Riviere ms]

**MARIA,** from Copenhagen to St Thomas in November 1687, arrived there on 24 March 1688. [DWI]

**MARIA VAN AMSTERDAM,** [Mary of Amsterdam], was
   seized by the authorities in Barbados in 1652.
   [Cal.SP.Col.XI.380]

**MARIAGE ROYALE DE LA ROCHELLE,** [Royal
   Marriage of La Rochelle], 50 tons, master J. Fallou, from
   La Rochelle, France, to Cape Breton in 1662. [La
   Rochelle Library, Cherbonnier ms]

**MARIE DE ST JEAN DE LUZ,** [Mary of St John of Luz], 60
   tons, at Cape Breton in 1629. [NA.CO1.5#50]

**MARIE,** 86 tons, master P. Metifeu, arrived in Quebec in
   August 1643. [NAC]

**MARIE DE BROUAGE,** [Mary of Brouage], 400 tons, master
   Jacques Pingault, from La Rochelle, France, to
   Newfoundland and Acadia in 1661, arrived in Quebec in
   1661. [La Rochelle Library, Moreau ms][NAC]

**MARIE DE ROYAN,** [Mary of Royan], 40 tons, from
   Bordeaux, France, to Quebec and return in 1685.
   [Gironde Archives 6B71/68, 6B291, 6B1029]

**MARIE,** 45 tons, master Nicolas Despot, from La Rochelle,
   France, to Port Royal, Acadia, and Chicoutimi to the
   West Indies in 1685. [Charente Maritime Archives
   B56837]

**MARIE,** from Marseilles, France, *with 79 Huguenot
   passengers* bound for St Domingo in September 1687,
   arrived there in February 1688. [HEA#224]

**MARIE OF BOSTON,** master James Small, arrived in Port
   Glasgow, Scotland, in July 1689 from Virginia; from
   Port Glasgow to Fyall in September 1689; master
   William Black, arrived in Port Glasgow on 27 February
   1691 from Maryland. [NAS.E72.19.14/15/21]

**MARIE DE LA ROCHELLE,** [Mary of La Rochelle], master
   Alain Durand, from France to Canada and the West
   Indies in 1690. [Gironde Archives 6B74/10, 6B295/115]

**MARIE OF ST MARY'S, MARYLAND,** master William Clark, from Port Glasgow, Scotland, to Virginia on 24 September 1691. [NAS.E72.19.22]

**MARIE DE BORDEAUX,** [Mary of Bordeaux], master Pierre Vigneau, from Bordeaux, France, to Quebec in 1698, captured by pirates off the island of St Pierre on the return voyage. [Gironde Archives 6B1091]

**MARIE – MARTHE,** master N. Ecussard, from France to Quebec, arrived there in July 1638. [NAC]

**MARIGOLD OF GLASGOW,** master Robert Gass, possibly from Barbados to Greenock, Scotland, in 1691. [NAS.RD3.78.32]

**MARIN,** from Brest, France, on 24 October 1698 bound for Louisiana. [ASC#181]

**MARSCHAL DONFLING,** master John Catt, from Pillau, Prussia, via Emden to Guinea and St Thomas, arrived there on 23 November 1686; master Gerrit Ver Beech, from Brandenburg, Germany, to St Thomas in the Virgin Islands in September 1687; from Emden, Germany, via Guinea to St Thomas in 1692. [DWI][RAK]

**MARTHA OF LONDON,** 120 tons, master Henry Taverner, from the West Indies to the River Clyde in Scotland, arrived at Newark, Dumbarton, on 29 January 1640. [Dumbarton Common Good Accounts, 1614-1660][NA.HCA.13/56. 426]

**MARTYN VAN RUSSEN OF MIDDELBURG,** 300 tons, master Leonard Johnson, from Middelburg, Zealand, in November 1660, via Africa to Jamaica, arriving there in February 1661, seized by HMS Diamond; at Jamaica in 1663. [DI.I/154][SPAWI.1663.461] [NA.HCA.Prizepapers, Libel#115/102]

**MARY,** master David Couston, from Leith, Scotland, *with passengers* to Barbados in May 1663. [Edinburgh Burgh Records, #186.13.4]

**MARY,** from Leith, Scotland, to Virginia in May 1671.
[RPCS.III.331]

**MARY,** 40 tons, master David Wading, with a crew of 8 men,
from Waterford, Ireland, to the Bay of Bulls,
Newfoundland, in 1684. [NA.CO1/55.239/246]

**MARY OF BOSTON,** a pink, master James Smith, when
sailing from Virginia to Glasgow, Scotland, was attacked
by a French privateer, but arrived in Port Glasgow in
July 1689. [NAS.E72.19.14][RPCS.XIII.477]

**MARY,** master John Pindar, from New Hampshire to Lisbon,
Portugal, in March 1700. [SPAWI.1700/354ii]

**MARYA EN JAN,** [Mary and John], master Francois
Hurdidge, from Virginia to Hellevoetsluis, the
Netherlands, in 1644. [GAR.ONA.171.22.29]

**MARYLAND MERCHANT OF BRISTOL,** Captain Raxsell,
arrived in Kinsale, Ireland, in May 1669 when bound for
Bristol, England, from Virginia. [Cal.SPIre.1669/123]

**MATHIEU DE LA ROCHELLE,** [Mathew of La Rochelle],
master Mathieu Augizeau, from France to the West
Indies and Canada in 1684. [Gironde Archives
6B70/120]

**MATTHEW AND FRANCIS OF LONDON,** 300 tons,
master Richard Bread, from Texel in the Netherlands
bound for Barbados in 1668. [ActsPCCol.1668/823]

**MAYFLOWER,** master William Richards, from Amsterdam,
Holland, to New Orange, in 1674; from New York via
London to Amsterdam in 1675. [GAA#3778]

**MAYFLOWER OF GLASGOW,** master Robert Johnstone,
from Port Glasgow, Scotland, bound for the West Indies
in October 1682; master Walter Noble, from Port
Glasgow to the Caribee Islands in March 1685; master
Thomas Stalker, arrived in Glasgow, Scotland, on 10
March 1686 from the West Indies. [NAS.E72.19.9/12]

**MAYFLOWER OF LIVERPOOL,** master John Martin, from Port Glasgow, Scotland, to the West Indies on 25 January 1682. [NAS.E72.19.6]

**MAYFLOWER OF BOSTON or NEW YORK or PRESTON,** master Henry Martin, arrived in Glasgow, Scotland, in June 1683 from Virginia; arrived in Glasgow in October 1683 from Barbados; from Glasgow in October 1683 bound for Virginia; from Port Glasgow to Virginia in October 1685. [NAS.E72.19.8]

**MAYFLOWER OF LONDON,** master Thomas Mooch, arrived in Port Glasgow, Scotland, during August 1689 from Maryland; master John Spurrill, from Scotland *with 108 passengers* to Barbados, arrived there on 5 December 1698. [NAS.E72.19.14][NA.CO3/13]

**MERCHANT OF GLASGOW,** master George Dredan, from Glasgow, Scotland, *with passengers* bound for the American Plantations in 1670. [RPCS.III.299/679]

**MERCHANTS ADVENTURE,** 400 tons, from Ireland to the West Indies in 1670. [ActsPCCol.1670/898]

**MERCHANTS ADVENTURE OF BELFAST,** master Moses Jones, arrived in Port Glasgow, Scotland, in September 1682 from Barbados. [NAS.E72.19.5]

**MERCHANTS GOODWILL,** from Ireland to Newfoundland in 1691. [ActsPCCol.16.7.1691]

**MERCURIUS,** [Mercury], master Jan Hindrickson Lang, from Sweden *with 130 passengers* in 1655 bound for Nya Sverige, (New Sweden), arrived at Fort Christina on the Delaware River on 24 March 1656. [SSD#761]

**MERMAID OF LONDON,** master John Rodger, from Glasgow (?), Scotland, via the Orkney Islands to Virginia in 1698. [NAS.RD4.83.544]

**MICHAEL OF GALWAY,** at Montserrat in May 1673. [SPAWI.1673/1109]

**MIDDELBURGH VAN MIDDELBURGH,** [Middleburgh of Middleburgh], in the West Indies, 1632. [GAR.ONA.302.28.51]

**MOISE DE LA ROCHELLE,** [Moses of La Rochelle], 60 tons, master Pierre Jamin, from La Rochelle, France, to Acadia in 1658. [La Rochelle Archives, Savin ms/Teuleronm ms]

**MOISES OF CARDIFF,** 50 tons, arrived in Cardiff, Wales, from Newfoundland in 1600. [WPB#234]

**MORNING STAR,** master Andrew Baxter, from Dumbarton, Scotland, to Nova Scotia *with passengers* in April 1627. [RL]

**MOULIN D'OR,** [Golden Mill], master Pierre Jamin, arrived in Quebec during 1666; from Quebec on 18 October 1666 bound via Acadia for France. [NAC][DCB.I.467]

**MOUTON BLANC DE BORDEAUX,** [The White Sheep of Bordeaux], 300 tons, master Andre Chaviteau, from La Rochelle, France, to Quebec In 1674; master Pierre Gravouil, to Quebec in 1678; master Andre Chaviteau, to Quebec in 1689. [La Rochelle Archives, Teuleron ms; Charente Maritime B5673/B5675/B5680; La Rochelle, Droyneau ms]

**MOUTON,** [Sheep], from France to Canada in June 1677. [BN.Mel;anges de Colbert #174/395]

**MULET,** [Mule], from France *with passengers* to Canada in 1685. [BN.Collection Arnoul]

**NATIVITIE DE QUEBEC,** [Nativity of Quebec], master Jean Basset, from Le Havre, France, to Quebec, returning to La Rochelle, France, in 1672; master Thare Chaillaud, to Quebec in 1673; master Jean Bourdon Dhombourg, from Bordeaux, France, to Quebec in 1674 and in 1675. [Charente Maritime Archives.B5671/176; B5672/243; Bordeaux Archives. 1674/214-221; Quebec Archives, Becquet ms]

**NEGRO,** master John Lockier, from Dublin, Kinsale and Cork, Ireland, *with passengers* bound for Barbados, arrived in St Kitts in 1657. [NA.HCA.Exams.#71]

**NEPTUNE OF COPENHAGEN,** master Peter Lutzen, to St Kitts and Nevis during 1654-1655. [Cal.SPCol.XII.422]

**NEPTUNE,** master Herman Schroder, from Denmark to the West Indies in September 1674. [RAK]

**NEPTUNE DE LA ROCHELLE,** [Neptune of La Rochelle], master Jean Sibron, from La Rochelle, France, to Acadia in 1666; master Andre Chaviteau, from La Rochelle to Quebec in 1672. [Charente Maritime Archives, B5671/2/184; La Rochelle Archives, Riviere, Teuleron ms]

**NEPTUNUS,** [Neptune], master Maerten Williamszoon, to the West Indies in 1600; master Jacob Dircxzoon, from Rotterdam, Zealand, to Madeira in 1610. [GAR.ONA.8.121.399/ 47.175.251]

**NEPTUNUS,** [Neptune], in the West Indies, 1636. [GAR.ONA.302.256.516]

**NEUF OU ST JEAN,** 80 tons, master Jean Bourdet, arrived in Quebec on 14 July 1650. [NAC]

**NEUF OU ST SAUVEUR,** 150 tons, arrived in Quebec in August 1648; master .... Jammes, arrived in Quebec in August 1649. [NAC]

**NEW SUPPLY OF CHESTER,** master John Glover, from Glasgow, Scotland, to America in March 1684. [NAS.E72.19.12]

**NEWPORT,** 100 tons, master Edward Burwash, via Waterford, Ireland, to Montserrat in 1691. [ActsPCCol.1690/364/27]

**NEW YORK MERCHANT,** from Holland bound for New York in 1696. [ActsPCCol.1696#577/27]

**NICHOLAS OF MILBROOK,** arrived in Milford, Wales, from Newfoundland in 1603. [WPB#234]

**NICHOLAS OF JERSEY**, master Thomas Badinell, from Jersey in the Channel Islands to Virginia in 1671. [ActsPCCol.1671/926]

**NICOLAS,** from France to Quebec, arrived there in July 1637. [NAC]

**NICOLAS JAN VAN VLISSINGEN,** [Nicolas John of Flushing], from Findhorn, Morayshire, Scotland, to Surinam in 1684, possibly arrived there on 23 March 1685. [NAS.E72.11.9; RH15.106.567/1]

**NIEUW AMSTEL,** [New Amstel], a galliot, master Augustinus Heermans, from Curacao to Nieuw Amsterdam, 1659. [DI.I/140]

**NIEUW JORCK,** [New York], master Claes Hendricksz. Lock, from Amsterdam, Holland, *with passengers* in April 1668 to Nieuw Amsterdam, from there to the Netherlands in June 1668. [CJR#398][GAA#2845]

**NIEUW NEDERLANDT,** [Nieuw Nederland], master Cornelis Jacobszoon May, from Amsterdam, Holland, on 30 March 1624 *with 30 Walloon families and Huguenots* bound for the Nieuw Nederland, arrived at the North (Hudson) River in June 1624, returned to Holland in October 1624; from the Nieuw Nederland to Amsterdam in 1632. [GAA.NA667/27; NA306/119-123] [DNY#1/149]

**NIEUW NEDERLANDSCHE FORTUYN,** [New Netherlands Fortune], from Amsterdam, Holland, *with 70 passengers* bound for Staten Island, Nieuw Nederland, in August 1650. [DNY#1/528]

**NIEUW SWOL,** [New Swol], from Amsterdam, Holland, bound for the Nieuw Nederland in 1647. [NMM]

**NIEUW WALCHEREN,** [New Walcheren], master Luke Pole, at Tobago, (alias New Walcheren), in 1636. [SPAWI.1673/1085]

**NIGHTINGALE OF HULL,** master John Hobson, arrived in Kirkcaldy, Fife, Scotland, from "Wayrter, Maryland in Virginia", on 17 May 1673. [NAS.E72.9.8/2]

**NOIR VAN HOLLAND,** master Pierre Fillye, from Dieppe, France, *with 51 indentured servants* bound for Quebec in 1664, arrived there in May 1664. [La Rochelle Archives, Cherbonnier ms]

**NOM DE JESUS DE LA ROCHELLE,** [Name of Jesus of La Rochelle], master Pierre Durand, from La Rochelle, France, to Quebec in 1686; master Nicolas Blacquebot, from La Rochelle to Quebec in 1688; master Charles Chaviteau, from La Rochelle to Quebec and the West Indies in 1689. [Charente Maritime Archives B235, B5684; Gironde Archives 6B73]

**NOORTHOLLANT,** [The North Holland], in the West Indies, 1639. [GAR.ONA.271.95.137]

**NOTRE DAME,** [Our Lady], 250 tons, arrived in Quebec in August 1643; arrived in Quebec in June 1644; master Charles Legarder de Tilly, from France to Quebec and Montreal, arrived in August 1645; master C. Legardeur de Tilly, arrived in Quebec in September 1646; arrived in Quebec in August 1647; arrived in Quebec in August 1648; arrived in Quebec in August 1649. [NAC]

**NOTRE DAME DE BONNE NOUVRELLE,** 200 tons, master Jacques Jamain, arrived in Quebec during 1662. [NAC]

**NOTRE DAME DE POSSESSION DE LA ROCHELLE,** [Our Lady of the Possession of La Rochelle], 60 tons, master Nicolas Blaetran, from France to Quebec and the West Indies in 1691, but was seized and taken to Boston, New England. [La Rochelle Archives, Riviere, Soulard ms]

**NOTRE DAME DE PROTECTION,** 150 tons, master Jean
Baptiste Mornant, from La Rochelle, France, to Canada
and Newfoundland in 1690. [Charente Maritime
Archives B5686]

**NOTRE DAME DE ROSAIRE DE SIBOURE,** [Our Lady of
the Rosary of Siboure], 160 tons, master ...Congerie,
from La Rochelle, France, via Quebec to the West Indies
in 1691. [Charente Maritime Archives B235]

**NOUVELLE FRANCE DE LA ROCHELLE,** [New France
of La Rochelle], 300 tons, master Andre Chaviteau, from
France to Quebec in 1667, returned under master ....
Tadourneau in 1668; master Alain Durant, from La
Rochelle, France, to Canada in 1670. [La Rochelle
Archives, Teuleron 3E1370; BN.Melanges de Colbert,
#176]

**O'BRIAN OF DUBLIN,** possibly from Cork bound for
Antigua, was seized by HMS Dartmouth and tried before
the Admiralty Court of Nevis in April 1686.
[SPAWI.1686/621/910/931]

**OLD HEAD OF KINSALE,** master Robert Barker, from
Barbados to the Leeward Islands in January 1679; from
Carolina and Virginia to Antigua in 1684. [Hotten,
p.413][NA.C24/1095]

**OLIN TACK,** master Daniel Pets, from Brandenburg,
Germany, to St Thomas, Virgin Islands, in March 1698.
[RAK]

**OLIVE BRANCH,** master William Jamieson, from Leith,
Scotland, *with passengers* bound for Darien on the
Isthmus of Panama in 1699. [NAS.CC8.8.83]

**ORANAENBURG,** from Brandenburg, Germany, to St
Thomas, Virgin Islands, in March 1698. [RAK]

**ORANGE,** 250 tons, from France to Quebec in 1665, arrived
there on 29 July 1665; master .....Raymond, from La
Rochelle, France, to Quebec in 1667; 280 tons, master

Guillaume Hurtin, from La Rochelle to Acadia in 1671. [BN #JA13/175][La Rochelle Archives, Teuleron#68] [DCB.I.62]

**ORANGE OF NORTH YARMOUTH,** master .... Barton, arrived in Kinsale, Ireland, from Barbados in June 1669 bound for Holland. [CalSPIreland.1669/736]

**ORANJEBOOM VAN AMSTERDAM,** [Orange Tree of Amsterdam], 150 tons, from Amsterdam, Holland, *with passengers* bound via Plymouth, England, for the Nieuw Nederland in 1625. [ActsPCCol.1625/133][DNY#III/12]

**ORANJEBOOM,** [Orange Tree], master Jan Alewijns, in the West Indies, 1634. [GAR.ONA.322.7.14]

**ORANJEBOOM VAN MIDDELBURG,** [Orange Tree of Middleburg], 150 tons, master .... Downeman, from St Kitts bound for the Netherlands, but captured and taken to Plymouth, England, in 1662; from Amsterdam, Holland, via England to New York and return in 1667-1668. [ActsPCCol.1662/579][GAA#2225/2845][NMM]

**ORANJIEN,** from Middelburg, Zealand, to Brazil on 31 October 1629. [GAR.ONA.204.16.24]

**ORATAINE GALLEY,** master Bartholemew Borman, from Stade, Germany, to the Canary Islands in 1705. [Cal.SPDom.SP44/1393/95]

**ORMONDE OF DUBLIN,** a frigate, master Henry Brann, arrived in Kinsale, Ireland, on 9 August 1669 from Barbados bound for Holland; from Kinsale to Barbados and the Leeward Islands in November 1674. [Cal.SPIre.1669/213][SPDom.1674/417]

**ORN,** [Eagle], master Jan Jansson Bockhorn, from Sweden *with 250 passengers* bound for Nya Sverige, (New Sweden), in 1654, arrived in the South (Delaware) River on 21 May 1654. [SSD#761][PA.V.253]

**PASSEMOY,** 250 tons, arrived in Quebec on 13 October 1651, arrived in Quebec in 1652. [NAC]

**PATRIARCHE ABRAHAM,** [Patriarch Abraham], master
Guillaume Poulet, arrived in Quebec in 1653; arrived in
Quebec in 1654; arrived in Quebec in 1655. [NAC]

**PELICAN,** arrived in St Thomas *with passengers* on 29 March
1673; returned to Copenhagen, Denmark, on 25 October
1673 from the West Indies. [DWI][RAK]

**PELICAN OF GLASGOW,** master James Gibson, from Port
Glasgow, Scotland, *with 180 passengers* to Carolina on
19 June 1684. [RPCS.IX.208][NAS.E72.19.9]

**PETIT ST JEAN,** [Little St John], 200 tons, master Rene
Boutin, from France to Quebec in 1654; arrived in
Quebec in 1663 from France . [NAC]

**PHOENIX OF LEITH,** master James Gibson, from Leith,
Scotland, *with passengers* bound for Virginia in May
1666, arrived there before November 1666.
[NAS.HH#1/11][ECA][York County Records, Virginia]

**PHOENIX OF LONDON,** master Leonard Haynes, from La
Rochelle, France, in July 1675 bound for Newfoundland
and Virginia, landed at Cherrystone Creek, Virginia.
[SPAWI.1681/183]

**PHOENIX,** master Mathew Shaw, arrived in the Delaware
River *with passengers* possibly from Dublin, Ireland, in
1677. [PMHB#9]

**PILGRIM OF DARTMOUTH,** master John Ewins, from
Newfoundland bound for Averro, Portugal, but captured
by the Spanish in July 1667. [PCCol.1668/760]

**PLAIN DEALING OF COLERAINE,** a pink, possibly from
America to Greenock, Scotland, in 1691.
[NAS.RD3.73.32]

**PLANTER,** from Virginia to the Netherlands in 1646.
[GAR.ONA.334.231.563]

**PLOUGH OF LONDON,** master Robert Bramble, from St Kitts to Kinsale, Ireland, in 1637. [NAS.HCA.13/53/302]

**POLI,** from France to Quebec in 1692; master Pierre Le Moyne d'Iberville, arrived in Quebec in 1693. [ASC#180][NAC]

**POMEGRANATE OF LONDON,** a 69 ton pink, master Richard Griffin, from Ireland to Barbados, arrived there on 25 March 1699. [NA.CO333/13]

**POSTILLION,** master Vincent de Clerck, from Brandenburg, Germany, to St Thomas, Virgin Islands, in October 1693. [RAK]

**PRESTON,** 100 tons, master John Crowther, from Plymouth, England, via Cork, Ireland, to Barbados, Virginia, and return in 1698. [NA.Exams.Vol.81]

**PRIMROSE,** from Amsterdam, Holland, to Barbados in 1670.[BA:RB6/8/49]

**PRINCE GUILLAUME,** [Prince William], 200 tons, master Jacques Jamain from France to Quebec in 1658; master Guillaume Heurtin, from France to Quebec in 1659. [NAC]

**PRINCE MAURICE DE LA ROCHELLE,** [Prince Maurice of La Rochelle], from La Rochelle, France, to the West Indies in 1670; master Pierre Heraud, from France to Quebec in 1671; master Jean Garos, from La Rochelle to the West Indies in 1672; master Jean Du Halde, from La Rochelle to Quebec in 1673; from La Rochelle to the West Indies in 1675; master Elie Mouliot, from La Rochelle to Quebec in 1677; master J. Blondet, from France to Acadia and Quebec in 1678; master Etienne Archambeau, from La Rochelle to Quebec and the West Indies in 1685. [Charente Maritime Archives, B5672/3/6; La Rochelle Archives, Teuleron.192/8419/38/31]

**PRINCESS OF DENMARK,** master Jan Waegenear, from Gluckstad to St Thomas in the Virgin Islands in July 1685. [RAK]

**PRINCESSE,** [The Princess], from Nieuw Amsterdam *with passengers* to Holland on 16 August 1647. [VH#1/37]

**PRINS,** [The Prince], from the Netherlands to Barbados in 1649. [DNY#1/387]

**PRINS HENRICK TE PAERT,** master Adriaan Jacobszoon Muts, from Pernambuco and St Kitts to the Netherlands in 1647. [GAR.ONA.87.61.117]

**PRINS MAURITS,** [Prince Maurice], from the Netherlands to Pernambuco in 1639; master Dirck Cornelissen, from Amsterdam, Holland, *with 112 passengers, possibly including Waldensians* to the Nieuw Nederland on 21 December 1656, landed near Fort Casimir on 21 April 1657. [GAR.ONA.135.254.347][DNY#2/4][PA.2.7/497]

**PRINS WILLEM,** [Prince William], from Amsterdam, Holland, to the Nieuw Nederland in 1648; at Nieuw Amsterdam in 1659. [NMM][CJR#198]

**PRINSES,** [Princess], from the Netherlands to the Nieuw Nederland via Curacao (?) in August 1646, arrived in May 1647. [DNY#1/455]

**PRINSES AMELIA,** [Princess Amelia], from Amsterdam, Holland, bound for the Nieuw Nederland in 1647. [NMM]

**PRINTZ CHRISTIAN,** [Prince Christian], master Jacob Bonina, from Copenhagen, Denmark, to St Thomas, Virgin Islands, in November 1694. [RAK]

**PRINZ WILLEM VAN VLISSINGEN,** [Prince William of Flushing], 180 tons, from La Rochelle, France, *with a passengers* bound for Acadia, Boston, and elsewhere, in 1658, and also in 1659. [La Rochelle Archives, Savin ms; La Rochelle Library, Moreau#160]

**PROVIDENCE,** arrived in Newport News, Virginia, in April 1623 from Ireland. [NA.CO1/11#28]

**PROVIDENCE,** from Providence via New England and Newfoundland to Galway, Ireland, in 1640. [NA.HCA.13/56/416]

**PROVIDENCE OF LONDON,** master Thomas or George Swanley, from Kinsale, Ireland, *with passengers* bound for the Rappahannock River, Virginia, in 1653-1654. [NA.Inter-Regnum Book, Vol.98/338; HCA.Libels#112/131; Cal.SPCol.Vol.XII/407]

**PROVIDENCE OF KINSALE,** arrived in Kinsale, Ireland, in 1669 from Antigua and Montserrat. [Cal.SPIre.1669/266]

**PROVIDENCE DE ST JEAN DE LUZ,** 80 tons, from La Rochelle, France, to Acadia and the West Indies in 1671. [La Rochelle Archives, Teuleron]

**PROVIDENCE OF GLASGOW,** master John Anderson, arrived in Glasgow, Scotland, on 3 September 1672 from Antigua. [NAS.E72.10.3]

**PROVIDENCE OF LONDON,** master Roger Severn, from Accomack, Virginia, to Dublin, Ireland, in August 1678, arrived there on 20 November 1678; arrived in Somerset County, Maryland, in 1692 from Scotland. [NA.HCA#15/9][SPAWI.1692/2295]

**PROVIDENCE OF PISCADUA,** master Mark Hinckley, arrived in Glasgow, Scotland, from Virginia in September 1681; from Port Glasgow to Virginia on 8 November 1681; returned to Port Glasgow in June 1682 from Virginia; from Port Glasgow to Virginia on 13 July 1682. [NAS.E72.19.5/6]

**PROVIDENCE OF COLERAINE,** master Alexander Doick, arrived in Ayr, Scotland, from Virginia via Londonderry, Ireland, in 1685. [NAS.E72.3.16]

**PROVIDENCE OF BELFAST,** master John Lorimer, arrived in Port Glasgow during September 1689 from Montserrat. [NAS.E72.19.14]

**PROVIDENCE DE LA ROCHELLE,** [Providence of La Rochelle], 120 tons, master Jean Tesseron, from La Rochelle, France, on 22 June 1692 bound for Quebec but shipwrecked at Cul-de-Sac in 1692. [Bordeaux Archives, Loste ms][NAC]

**PROVIDENCE OF DUBLIN,** 160 tons, master John Hamilton, from Dublin, Ireland, *with passengers* bound for Virginia, arrived in the Rappahannock River, Virginia, on 30 March 1699; master Andrew Gregg, at Annapolis, Maryland, in July 1699; was seized by the colonial authorities. [SPAWI.1699/542, 586] [VAC:12.7.1699][XJVa#1/458]

**RACHEL AND JOHN OF LONDON,** from Kelburn, Ayrshire, Scotland, on 4 March 1686 bound for Antigua, arrived there on 15 May 1686, from Antigua on 27 July 1686 bound for Port Royal, South Carolina. [Misc.Bound Collection, W. C. Clements Library, University of Michigan]

**RAINBOW,** from Galway, Ireland, to the Caribee Islands in 1653-1654. [Cal.SPCol.XII.409]

**RAINBOW OF GLASGOW,** master Harry Hart, from Glasgow, Scotland, to the American Plantations in February 1671. [RPCS.II.299]

**RAMMEKENS,** master Nicolaas Everts, from the Nieuw Nederland via Barbados and Surinam to Essequibo in 1700. [SPAWI.1700.715]

**RANDELL DE ST MALO,** France, from Newfoundland in September 1627. [NAS.AC7.1.109]

**REBECCA OF DUBLIN,** master James Gollier, from Ayr, Scotland, to Barbados, Montserrat, and other places in the West Indies in 1642. [NAS.RD1.544.6]

**REBECCA,** master Thomas Williams, from New York to Amsterdam, Holland, in 1677-1678. [NMM]

**REBECCA,** master James Duncan, from Scotland to New
York in 1682. [NYDeeds, Liber#19B/66]

**REBECCA OF DUBLIN,** at Nevis, 1686. [SPAWI.1686/621]

**REBECCAH OF GALLOWAY,** seized by the colonial
authorities in Barbados in 1701. [SPAWI.1702/28]

**RECOVERY,** master John Allen, from Portpatrick, Scotland,
or Knockfergus, Ireland, *with 300 passengers* to the
West Indies in May 1656. [NA.SP25/77]

**RECOVERY OF MARYLAND,** master Henry Smith, arrived
in Greenock, Scotland, from America in 1691 and in
1692. [NAS.RD4.67.97; RD3.78.32]

**RENCONTRE DE LA ROCHELLE,** [The Encounter of La
Rochelle], master Pierre St Marc, from France to Quebec
and the West Indies in 1689; master Louis Aramy, from
France to Quebec and the West Indies in 1698. [La
Rochelle Archives, Berthelot ms; Gironde Archives,
6B73/66, 6B294]

**RENE,** 120 tons, master N. Pernet, arrived in Quebec in June
1641; arrived in Quebec in 1656. [NAC]

**RENEE MARIE DE ST GILLES,** 60 tons, master Pierre
Gravoil, from La Rochelle, France, to Port Royal in
Acadia and the West Indies in 1684. [Charente Maritime
Archives B5682]

**RICHMOND,** master ..... Forrester, from Kinsale, Ireland, to
Barbados in July 1667. [Cal.SPIreland.1667/139]

**RISING SUN,** master James Gibson, from Greenock,
Scotland, *with passengers* bound for Darien on the
Isthmus of Panama, on 20 September 1699, from there to
Charleston, South Carolina, where it was wrecked in
1700. [NAS.GD406]

**ROBERT OF KINSALE,** arrived in Kinsale, Ireland, from
Barbados in September 1667. [Cal.SPIreland.1667/467]

**ROBERT,** from Scotland to Carolina before 1688.
[NAS.GD393/79]

**ROBERT OF GLASGOW,** master Nathaniel Davis, from
Port Glasgow, Scotland, to Virginia on 5 March 1691.
[NAS.E72.15.22]

**ROBERT OF LONDONDERRY,** from Scotland to Virginia
in 1691. [NAS.GD3.5.805]

**RODE HANE,** [The Red Hen], from Denmark to the West
Indies in October 1687. [RAK]

**ROTTERDAM,** master Pieter Claeszoon, in the West Indies,
1608. [GAR.ONA.14.82.255]

**ROTTERDAM,** a yacht, in the West Indies, 1636.
[GAR.ONA.293.44.56]

**ROTTERDAM,** a fluit, to the Canary Islands and the West
Indies in 1698. [GAR.ONA.1244.148.468]

**ROYAEL CHAIRLES,** [Royal Charles], a warship, from the
Netherlands to the West Indies in 1667.
[GAR.ONA.238.98.199]

**ROYALE PAIX,** from La Rochelle, France, on 20 August
1699 bound for Port Royal in Acadia, arrived there on 13
October 1699. [ASC#176]

**SAEL,** from Amsterdam to Brazil, 1626.
[GAR.ONA.140.191.318]

**ST AGNES DE LA ROCHELLE,** [St Agnes of La Rochelle],
master Jean Monbeuil, from France to Quebec in 1679;
master Pierre Monbeuil, from La Rochelle to Quebec in
1682; master Joseph Vivier, from Bordeaux to Quebec in
1684. [Charente Maritime Archives, B5678, B5681]
[Gironde Archives, 6B290/6B1026][La Rochelle
Archives, Berthelot, Teuleron ms]

**ST ANDRE DE LA ROCHELLE,** [St Andrew of La
Rochelle], 300 tons, master Guillaume Poulet, from la

Rochelle, France, *with passengers* to Quebec on 29 June 1659, landed there on 7 September 1659. [La Rochelle Library, Moreau#185][DCB.I.458][NAC]

**ST ANDREW,** from Leith, Scotland, *with passengers* to Darien on the Isthmus of Panama on 14 July 1698. [NAS.GD406/B160/2/29]

**ST ANN VON HOLSTEIN,** [St Ann of Holstein], 250 tons, master Heindrich Reurs, from La Rochelle, France, to Quebec in 1668. [WMQ.LII.96][L Rochelle Archives, Teuleron#115]

**ST ANN OF GALWAY,** arrived in Kinsale, Ireland, on 14 July 1669 from Barbados when bound for London. [CSPIre]

**STE ANNE,** from France to Martinique in 1624. [LPA#44]

**STE ANNE,** from Quebec to France in 1668. [DCB.1.480]

**STE ANNE DE ST MALO,** [St Ann of St Malo], 35 tons, master Jacques Tanquet, from Newfoundland bound for St Malo, France, arrived in Portsmouth, England, in 1673. [ActsPCCol.1674/975]

**STE ANNE,** a French ship, arrived at Port Nelson, Hudson's Bay, in August 1682; 120 tons, from Hudson's Bay to France in 1691; master Jean La Grange, from La Rochelle, France, to Quebec and Hudson's bay in 1692. [SPAWI.1683/1456][Nat.Arch.Col.C11a/77,291] [Charente Maritime Archives, B5695]

**STE ANNE DE LA ROCHELLE,** [St Anne of La Rochelle], master Pierre Chaviteau, from Bordeaux, France, to Canada in 1687; master Jacques Chaviteau, from La Rochelle via Bordeaux to Quebec in 1689. [LaRochelle Archives, Groze; Gironde Archives, 72/68, 6B73/157, 6B295]

**STE ANNE,** from Quebec to Placentia, Newfoundland, on 18 August 1692. [OC]

**STE ANNE DE BORDEAUX,** [St Anne of Bordeaux], master Guillaume Moret, from Bordeaux, France, to Canada in 1693. [NAC]

**ST ANTOINE DE LA ROCHELLE,** [St Antony of La Rochelle], 140 tons, master Pierre Bataille, from Bordeaux, France, to Quebec in 1685. [Gironde Archives, 6B71/64, 6B291]

**ST ANTOINE DE LA ROCHELLE,** [St Antony of La Rochelle], 70 tons, master Claude Le Clerc, from La Rochelle, France, to Quebec in 1695. [Charente Maritime Archives, B235]

**ST BENINO,** master Cornelis Claeszoon Snoij or Wilhelm Westerhuysen, from Edam in the Netherlands, arrived in Newhaven, New England, in August 1647, later in the Nieuw Netherlands. [GAA#1080][DNY#1/3337, 461]

**ST CHARLES DE BAYONNE,** [St Charles of Bayonne], from France to Canada in 1669; from La Rochelle to Acadia in 1670. [B.N.Melanges de Colbert #151/176]

**ST CHARLES,** master Pierre Tharay, from La Rochelle, France, to Acadia in 1682. [Charente Maritime Archives, B5681]

**ST CLEMENT,** from France to Acadia in 1643; 120 tons, master J. Guyonneau, arrived in Quebec in June 1644. [BNF#200][DCB.I.504][PAC]

**ST DAVID VON LUBECK,** [St David of Lubeck], master ....Ire, from Havanna, Cuba, in 1630 *with passengers* bound for Plymouth, England, arrived there on 29 July 1630. [Cal.SPCol.V.119]

**ST DENNIS,** a French privateer, was captured by an English privateer and taken to Port Royal, Jamaica, in 1702. [SPAWI.1702/1056]

**ST ETIENNE,** [St Steven], 350 tons, master Sieur de Pont Grave, from Honfleur, France, on 24 April 1615 *with* *passengers* bound for Quebec, arrived there on 26 June 1615. [VSC]

**ST ETIENNE,** [St Steven], 180 tons, from France via Gambia bound for the French islands in America on 30 March 1672, but seized by the English in Guinea. [SPAWI.1673/1111]

**STE FAMILLE DE LA ROCHELLE,** [Holy Family of La Rochelle], 80 tons, master Charles Francois, from La Rochelle, France, to Canada and the West Indies in 1690. [Gironde Archives, 6B74/18; La Rochelle Archives, Martin ms]

**ST FRANCIS VAN AMSTERDAM,** [St Francis of Amsterdam], master Henry Blasé, arrived at Milford in Wales during September 1638 with a cargo of tobacco. [NA.HCA.13/242/2]

**ST FRANCOIS,** 70 tons, possibly from Fecamp, France, to Newfoundland in March 1632, but captured on the return voyage and taken to Valentia in Ireland. [NA.HCA.13/50/291]

**ST FRANCOIS,** [St Francis], 130 tons, master J. Barraud, arrived in Quebec in July 1642; from France to Quebec in 1643. [NAC]

**ST FRANCOIS OU BON,** 90 tons, arrived in Quebec in August 1647. [NAC]

**ST FRANCOIS,** from La Rochelle, France, on 24 July 1684 *with passengers* bound for the Mississippi, arrived in Haiti in December 1684, later captured by the Spanish in the Caribbean Sea. [DCB.I.180]

**ST FRANCOIS DE LA ROCHELLE,** [St Francis of La Rochelle], 120 tons, master Francois Audiere, from La Rochelle, France, to Quebec and the West Indies in 1687; master Pierre Durand, from La Rochelle to Quebec and the West Indies in 1690. [Charente Maritime Archives, B235/139, B5685/6]

**ST FRANCOIS DE PAUL DE LA ROCHELLE,** [St Francis de Paul of La Rochelle], 120 tons, master Pierre Durand, from La Rochelle, France, via Bordeaux to Quebec and Martinique in 1690; master Michel Gravouil, to Quebec and Martinique in 1691; master Duhulque, to Plaisance, Newfoundland, in 1693. [Gironde Archives 6B74/14, 6B295/125; Charente Maritime Archives B235, B5686; La Rochelle Archives, Riviere and Soulard]

**ST FRANCOIS XAVIER DE QUEBEC,** [St Francis Xavier of Quebec], 150 tons, master J. F. Bourdon Dombourg, from La Rochelle, France, to Quebec in 1680. [Charente Maritime Archives, B5679]

**ST GEORGE,** master ...Lord, arrived in Kinsale, Ireland, from the West Indies in June 1667. [Cal.SPIreland, 1667/390]

**ST GEORGE OF LONDON,** from Spithead on 7 October 1677, via Waterford, Ireland, *with 180 passengers* bound for Maryland, arrived there by 1 November 1678. [SPDom.19/393][MSA.L.O.Patents#15/553]

**ST GEORGES,** [St George], arrived in Quebec in August 1648. [NAC]

**ST HELENE DE LA ROCHELLE,** [St Helen of La Rochelle], 120 tons, master Andre Chaviteau, from La Rochelle, France, to Quebec in 1670, also in 1672. [Charente Maritime Archives, B5669; La Rochelle Archives, Droyneau ms]

**ST HONORE DE LA ROCHELLE,** 150 tons, from New France to La Rochelle, France, in 1683; master Zacharie Aurilleau, from Bordeaux, France, to Canada in 1687. [DCB.I.179][Gironde Archives 6B72/78-81]

**ST JACOB,** [St James], from Enkhuizen, the Netherlands, to Madeira in 1627; master Jacob Huygen, from Madeira bound for the Netherlands in 1634; master Cornelis Jansz. Schellinger, from the Netherlands *with 100 passengers* to Pernambuco in 1640; master Jacob Pieterszoon Sort, from the Netherlands to Brazil in 1641;

master Haye Janszoon, from the Netherlands to the
Nieuw Nederland in 1646; master Pieter Luckassen,
from Amsterdam, Holland, *with passengers* in May 1663
bound for the Nieuw Nederland, arrived in New Amstel
in July 1663; from the Nieuw Nederland in 1663 bound
for Amsterdam; from the Nieuw Nederland on 28 August
1664 bound for the Netherlands; from Nieuw Amsterdam
on 6 November 1664 bound for the Netherlands.
[GAR.ONA.140.334.557/208.1.1/86.183.328/
329.169.362/734b/80/][DNY#2/230, 466, 467]
[PA.2.7/704]

ST JACOB VAN MIDDELBURG, [St James of
Middleburgh], from Zealand bound for the Canary
Islands in 1656 when captured by the <u>Weymouth</u> and
taken to Leith, Scotland. [NAS.AC2/1]

ST JACOB VON STADEN, [St James of Staden], from
Dublin, Ireland, to Barbados and Antigua in 1674. [Acts
PCCol#1038/1]

ST JACOB, [St James], master Jacques Vivien, from La
Rochelle, France, via Bordeaux, bound for Canada and
the West Indies in 1692. [Charente Maritime Archives
B5687/8]

ST JACOB, [St James], a French prize ship captured and taken
to Massachusetts in 1693. [SPAWI.1694/826-7]

ST JACQUES, [St James], master The Chevalier de la Roche
Jacquelin, arrived in Quebec during July 1635; master ..
Ancelot, arrived in Quebec in August 1639 also in
August 1640. [NAC]

ST JAGO OF NEW ENGLAND, [St James of New England],
returned to New England in 1695.
[ActsPCCol.1695/577-13]

ST JAN, [St John], in the West Indies, 1644.
[GAR.ONA332.85.174]

ST JAN, [St John], master Adriaen Blaes van der Veer, from
the Netherlands via West Africa to Tobago and Curacao

in 1651; from Guinea, on 29 October 1659, via Tobago
to Curacao arriving on 29 October 1659.
[NYCol.MS#17/52][DI.I/145]

ST JAN BAPTISTA, [St John the Baptist], master Pieter
Syboutsz., from Madeira bound for Hamburg, Germany,
and Rotterdam, Zealand, in 1623.
[GAR.ONA.78.156.324]

ST JAN BAPTIST, [St John the Baptist], a Dutch vessel
which was seized off New England by the English in
1655. [NA.Inter-Regnum Entry Book, CIV.188]

ST JAN BAPTIST, [St John the Baptist], master Symon
Claeszoon, from Amsterdam, Holland, bound for the
Nieuw Nederland in 1658; master Jan Bergen, from the
Nederland *with 9 passengers* bound for the Nieuw
Nederland, arrived in Nieuw Amsterdam on 6 August
1661. [DNY#2/452-460]

ST JAN BAPTISTA, [St John the Baptist], arrived in the
Nieuw Nederland on 6 August 1661, from there on 18
October 1661 bound for the Netherlands; from New
York to the Netherlands in 1683.
[CJR#260][CMMR#142]

ST JAN BAPTIST VAN VLISSINGEN, [St John the Baptist
of Flushing], 150 tons, master Guillaume Hurtin, from
France, arrived in Quebec on 4 July 1662. [La Rochelle
Archives, Cherbonnier][NAC]

ST JAN BAPTIST VON HAMBURG, [St John the Baptist of
Hamburg], at Nevis in 1668. [SPAWI.1668/1893]

ST JAN BATTISTO, from Amsterdam, Holland, to
Newfoundland in 1653. [GAA.NA1664/105-6]

ST JAN VAN AMSTERDAM, [St John of Amsterdam], a
Dutch privateer at Curacao in 1670.
[ActsPCCol.1670/901, 906]

ST JEAN, [St John], from Honfleur, France, in 1600 bound for
Tadoussac. [DCB.I.209]

**ST JEAN,** [St John], 160 tons, master Pierre de Nesle, arrived in Quebec on 22 May 1633; from France to Acadia *with 12 passengers* in 1636. [NAC][DCB.I.442]

**ST JEAN DE NORMANDIE,** [St John of Normandy], 100 tons, master Elie Raymond, arrived in Quebec in 1660. [NAC]

**ST JEAN DE BORDEAUX,** [St John of Bordeaux], 200 tons, master Pierre Guillebaud, from France to Quebec in 1671. [WMQ.LII.1/96]

**ST JEAN DE LA ROCHELLE,** [St John of La Rochelle], 150 tons, master Pierre Denys de Bonadventure, from France to Hudson's Bay and Canada in 1689; master Jean Chauvet, from Bordeaux to Quebec in 1691; master Sebastien Morval, from La Rochelle to Quebec in 1695. [La Rochelle Archives, Riviers and Soullard#14; Charente Maritime Archives, B235, 330-339]

**ST JEAN DE NANTES,** [St John of Nantes], a merchant vessel, was captured by an English privateer and taken to Port Royal, Jamaica, in 1702. [SPAWI.1702/1056]

**ST JEAN BAPTISTE DE DIEPPE,** [St John the Baptist of Dieppe], 300 tons, master Pierre Le Moyne, from France to Quebec *with 150 indentured servants* in 1664; master Pierre Fillye, *with 212 passengers* bound for Quebec in 1665; to Canada *with passengers* in 1666, arrived in Quebec in 1666; from Quebec bound for Dieppe, France, arrived there in January 1672. [La Rochelle Archives, Cherbonnier; Charente Maritime Archives B5667] [DCB.I.249][NAC]

**ST JEHAN,** from Port Royal, Acadia, to France via England in 1632; from France to Acadia in 1633. [BNF#193/194]

**ST JOHN,** arrived in Nieuw Amsterdam in 1628 from Africa. [VDV]

**ST JOHN OF LEITH,** from Leith, Scotland, *with passengers*
bound for the American Plantations in 1674.
[RPCS.IV.144/608]

**ST JOHN OF DUBLIN,** master Peter Lawrence, was seized in
New England during 1680. [SPAWI.1680/1625]

**ST JOHN BAPTIST,** a 500 ton Swedish ship, in Virginia
during 1666, its third voyage there.
[ActsPCCol.1666/687]

**ST JORIS,** [St George], from Curacao to Amsterdam, Holland,
in February 1660. [DI.I/150]

**ST JOSEPH,** Captain Bontemps, from Dieppe, France, on 4
May 1639 *with passengers* bound for Quebec, arrived at
Tadoussac on 31 July 1639. [DCB.I.205/348][NAC]

**ST JOSEPH,** 350 tons, master Jean Bouchier, arrived in
Quebec on 13 October 1651. [NAC]

**ST JOSEPH DE LA ROCHELLE,** [St Joseph of La
Rochelle], 300 tons, master Fabien Marot, from La
Rochelle, France, *with indentured servants* to Quebec in
1658; master Jean Tourneau, from La Rochelle *with
indentured servants* to Quebec in 1666. [NAC]
[La Rochelle Archives, Teuleron, Cherbonnier]

**ST JOSEPH,** master Pierre Estelle, from Tortuga bound for
Lisbon, Portugal, or La Rochelle, France, in March 1670,
the crew mutinied and took the ship to Boston, New
England. [SPAWI.1672/1007]

**ST JOSEPH DE BORDEAUX,** [St Joseph of Bordeaux],
master Pierre Riviere, from Bordeaux, France, to Quebec
in 1684; master Michel Paquinel, from Bordeaux to
Quebec, Acadia, and Newfoundland in 1686; master
Joseph Trebuchet, from Bordeaux to Quebec in 1688.
[Bordeaux Archives, Ferrand, Loste; Gironde Archives,
6B70/115, 6B72/149, 6B290, 294/15, 6B1045, Ferand,
Parran, Dufau]

**ST JOSEPH DE LA ROCHELLE,** [St Joseph of La
Rochelle], master Jean Couillandeau, from La Rochelle
and Bordeaux, France, to Quebec in 1692, 1693, and
1694, seized by a Jamaican privateer in 1694. [Charente
Maritime Archives, B235/B5687-8; La Rochelle
Archives, Grenot; Bordeaux Archives, Lalanne]

**ST LAURENS,** [St Laurence], master Claes Janszoon Burgh,
from Madeira bound for the Netherlands in 1640.
[GAR.ONA.152.4.21]

**ST LAURENS VON LUBECK,** [St Lawrence of Lubeck],
from Dunbarton, Scotland, *with 72 passengers* to Nova
Scotia in 1628. [DCB.I.54]

**ST LAWRENCE OF NORTH BERGEN,** trading with
Virginia or Barbados in 1674. [PCCol.1674/1006]

**ST LEO,** from Newfoundland to France in 1626, captured by
an English ship and taken to Dartmouth, England. [Acts
PCCol.1626/179]

**ST LOUIS,** master Michel Cande, from La Rochelle, France,
to Acadia and Quebec in 1684; from La Rochelle to
Acadia in 1685, 1686 and 1687. [Charente Maritime
Archives B5682/B5685; La Rochelle Archives,
Berthelot]

**ST LOUIS DE LA ROCHELLE,** [St Louis of La Rochelle],
250 tons, arrived at Chedabucto, Canada, on 14 July
1688. [ASC#207]

**ST LOUIS,** master Nicolas Egron, from La Rochelle, France,
to Quebec in 1693; master Salomon Benesteau, from
Bordeaux to Quebec and the West Indies in 1695; master
Jean Benesteau, from Bordeaux *with a passengers* to
Quebec and the West Indies in 1696. [Gironde Archives
6B76/95, 6B77/95, 6B297; Charente Maritime Archives,
B235/273/336, B5692; Bordeaux Archives, Cazenove,
Lalanne]

**ST LOUIS DE LA ROCHELLE,** [St Louis of La Rochelle],
70 tons, master Pierre Aereaud, from La Rochelle,

France, to Quebec and the West Indies in 1699. [La Rochelle Archives]

**ST MAERTEN,** [St Martin], from the Netherlands to the Nieuw Nederland in 1633. [DNY#1/432]

**ST MAERTEN VAN MIDDELBURCH,** [St Martin of Middleburgh], in the West Indies, 1638. [GAR.ONA.326.34.75]

**ST MATHIEU DE LA ROCHELLE,** [St Matthew of La Rochelle], master Etienne Augizeau, from La Rochelle, France, to Quebec and the West Indies in 1684; master Charles Chaviteau, from Bordeaux, *with a passenger,* to Quebec in 1686; master Matieu Augizeau, from La Rochelle via Bordeaux to Quebec and the West Indies in 1689; master Salomon Benesteau, from La Rochelle via Bordeaux to Quebec in 1690, also in 1691. [Charente Maritime Archives, B235, B5682; Gironde Archives, 6B71/152, 6B73/61, 6B74/29, 6B291/130, 6B294, 295]

**ST MICHAEL OF SCARBOROUGH,** master Edward Johnston, from Leith, Scotland, *with passengers* bound for the West Indies in December 1678. [RPCS.VI.76]

**ST MICHEL,** [St Michael], 300 tons, master Francois Doublet, from Honfleur (?), France, bound for Iles de la Madelaine in April 1663, arrived at Ile de Brion in May 1663. [DCB.I.277]

**ST MICHEL DE LE HAVRE,** [St Michael of Le Havre], master David Descultot, from Le Havre, France, bound for Newfoundland in 1677 when attacked by a Dutch vessel. [BN.Melanges de Colbert#175/229]

**ST MICHEL DE LA ROCHELLE,** [St Michael of La Rochelle], 120 tons, master Louis Maheu, from La Rochelle, France, to Quebec in 1680. [Charente Maritime Archives, B5679/121]

**ST MICHIEL,** 240 tons, from Enkhuizen in the Netherlands to Newfoundland in 1623. [GAA.NA738/175-8]

ST MICHIEL VAN STEENWYCK EN BAYERT, [St
Michael of Steenwyck and Bayert], from New Orange or
Nieuw Amsterdam in the Nieuw Nederland, to
Amsterdam, Holland, in March 1674.
[CJR#454][GAA.NA#2629] [NMM]

ST NICOLAS, 80 tons, master J. Richard, arrived in Quebec
during July 1642; master Pierre Le Besson, arrived in
Quebec in 1653; arrived in Quebec in 1654. [NAC]

ST NICOLAS DE LA ROCHELLE, [St Nicolas of La
Rochelle], 150 tons, master Etienne Dolbecq, from La
Rochelle, France, via Bordeaux to Quebec and the West
Indies in 1689, in 1690, and in 1691. [Gironde Archives,
6B3/68, 6B294; Charente Maritime Archives, B235,
B5686]

ST PAUL DE QUEBEC, [St Paul of Quebec], master Nicolas
Noel, from Bordeaux, France, to Quebec and the West
Indies in 1689. [Gironde Archives, 6B73/63, 6B294]

ST PETER OF PLYMOUTH, with a crew of 30 men and 16
guns, from Galway, Ireland, to Barbados in 1666.
[ActsPCCol.1666/723.1]

ST PETER VON HAMBURG, [St Peter of Hamburg], 300
tons, master Jacob Heull, from La Rochelle, France, to
Quebec in 1669; master J. Boutin, from La Rochelle to
Quebec in 1670. [La Rochelle Archives, Droyneau;
French Colonial Archives, Paris, B2/67]

ST PETER OF NEW YORK, master John Dishington,
arrived in Leith, Scotland, during June 1692. see James
wale's testament, NAS.CC8.8.79]

ST PHILLIPE DE BORDEAUX, [St Phillip of Bordeaux],
master Phillipe Sage, from Bordeaux, France, to Quebec
and the West Indies in 1687; from Bordeaux *with a
passenger* to Quebec in 1688 but wrecked on 30
November 1688 during the return voyage. [Girodne
Archives, 6B72/73, 165, 6B294/31; Bordeaux Archives,
Cazenove]

ST PHILLIPPE, [St Phillip], master Willem Pieterszoon
Beynemaer, from Madeira to the Netherlands in 1611.
[GAR.ONA.48.89.163]

ST PIERRE, [St Peter], 150 tons, master Pierre Gregoire,
arrived in Quebec on 22 May 1633. [NAC]

ST PIERRE, [St Peter], from Broage, France, to Acadia in
1635. [DCB.I.642]

ST PIERRE, [St Peter], 80 tons, master G. Gincard, arrived in
Quebec in July 1642, [NAC]

ST PIERRE, [St Peter], 300 tons, master Gringoire, from La
Rochelle, France, to Quebec in 1661; master Pierre
Philie, arrived in Quebec in 1661; arrived in Quebec in
1662; arrived in Quebec in 1663 from France. [NAC]
[La Rochelle Archives, Cherbonnier]

ST PIERRE DE BAYONNE, [St Peter of Bayonne], from
Newfoundland bound for France when captured by an
English ship and taken to Dartmouth, England, in 1677;
master Pascato de Hiroyen, from La Rochelle to
Newfoundland, St Pierre, and Quebec in 1679.
[ActsPCCol.1626/179][La Rochelle Archives, Teuleron]

ST PIERRE DE LA ROCHELLE, [St Peter of La Rochelle],
master Pierre Bataille, from La Rochelle, France, *with
passengers* bound for Quebec in 1679 when wrecked
near Newfoundland. [Charente Maritime Archives
B5678]

ST PIERRE, [St Peter], a French ship which arrived at Port
Nelson, Hudson's Bay, in August 1682.
[SPAWI.1683/1456]

ST PIERRE DE BORDEAUX, [St Peter of Bordeaux], master
Pierre Le Breton, from Bordeaux, France, to Quebec and
the West Indies in 1684, and to Quebec in 1685.
[Gironde Archives, 6B70/118, 6BB71/170, 6B290;
Bordeaux Archives, Ferrand/103]

**ST PIERRE DE BORDEAUX,** [St Peter of Bordeaux]
(formerly the Sara van Amsterdam), 150 tons, master
Jacques Dupeux, from Bordeaux, France, *with
passengers* to Quebec in 1689. [Gironde Archives,
6B73/118, 6B295, 6B1063; Bordeaux Archives,
Ferrand/72]

**ST PIERRE DE BAYONNE,** [St Peter of Bayonne], 160 tons,
captured at sea off Canada and taken to New York in
1690. [NA.HCA.Mauritz V. Flypson, 1692]

**ST PIETER,** [St Peter], master Cornelis Rijser, from
Amsterdam, Holland, to the "Terra Nova" in May 1611.
[GAA][NNC#18]

**ST PIETER,** from the Netherlands to Newfoundland, then to
England and back to Newfoundland in 1627.
[GAA.NA693/28]

**ST PIETER,** [St Peter], master Dirck Cornelis Kint, from
Madeira and the Canary Islands to Nieuwhaven, the
Netherlands in 1635; master Floris Jansz van der Graft,
from the Maas, Zealand, to Pernambuco and St Kitts,
1641; master Maerten Gerrebrants, from the Maas to
Virginia in 1647.
[GAR.ONA.323.117.273/ 165.97.158/323.157.391/
86.218.404/ 154.36.68]

**ST PIETER,** [St Peter], master Simon Janssen, from
Amsterdam, Holland, via Bermuda to the Nieuw
Nederland in 1645; from Amsterdam *with 9 passengers*
bound for the Nieuw Netherlands, arrived in Nieuw
Amsterdam on 19 February 1664. [DNY#1/174; 2/230,
467][HH#166]

**ST PIETER VAN GRONNICK,** [St Peter of Gronnick],
master Christian Eluez, from Holland in August 1662
bound for St Kitts but was captured by an English vessel
and taken to Montserrat. [ActsPCCol.1665/658]

**ST PIETER,** from the Netherlands to New York, arrived there
in October 1680. [CMR#40]

**ST SAUVEUR OU NEUF,** 150 tons, master Jean Paul
    Godefray, from France to Quebec in September 1644 and
    1646. [NAC]

**ST SEBASTIEN,** masters Guillaume and Jean Polet, from
    France to Quebec in 1656/57; arrived in Quebec in 1658;
    from France on 24 May 1665 bound for Quebec, arrived
    there by 12 September 1665; from La Rochelle, France,
    to Canada in 1666; from La Rochelle *with passengers* to
    Acadia in September 1670. [NAC][DCB.I.62/399/615]
    [BN.Melanges de Colbert#136; Cinq Cents de Colbert#
    125-127]

**ST SIMON DE BORDEAUX,** [St Simon of Bordeaux], 80
    tons, master Jacques Arnaud, from Bordeaux, France, to
    Quebec in 1672, also in 1673. [Bordeaux Archives,
    Ferrand/151, 1243]

**ST THOMAS,** master Thomas Shadlock, from Rotterdam,
    Zealand, to Madeira in 1612. [GAR.ONA.48.142.262]

**ST THOMAS,** a galliot, arrived in St Thomas, on 2 June 1675
    *with passengers*; from Copenhagen, Denmark, to St
    Thomas, Virgin Islands, in 1692; from the Danish West
    Indies to Copenhagen in 1697. [DWI#386]

**ST TONIS VAN DELFT,** in the West Indies, 1636.
    [GAR.ONA.293.56.72]

**ST VINCENT,** a yacht, master Bertel Bochelman, from
    Denmark to the West Indies in September 1674. [RAK]

**SALAMANDER,** master Thomas Wiltschildt, from
    Brandenburg, Germany, to St Thomas, Virgin Islands, in
    August 1690. [RAK][DWI]

**SALAMANDER VAN VLISSINGEN,** [Salamander of
    Flushing], master Michael de Ruyter, from the
    Netherlands to Barbados and the Caribee Islands in 1651.
    [NA.HCA.30/549]

**SALAMANDER VON BRANDENBURG,** [Salamander of Brandenburg], master Marcellus Cock, to Piscataqua, New England, in 1681. [SPAWI.1681/242]

**SALEM,** from the Texel, Holland, *with passengers* bound for Tortuga on 12 December 1630, but captured by Dunkirk pirates. [NMM]

**SALISBURY OF BOSTON,** master Andrew Doberry, arrived in Port Glasgow, Scotland, on 21 August 1689 from Virginia; from Port Glasgow to Madeira in September 1689. [NAS.E72.19.14/15]

**SALLEMANDE,** master ...Deschenes, from France on 5 April 1620, arrived in Quebec on 11 July 1620. [DCB.I.386]

**SALMOND OF CHESTER,** master John Glover, from Glasgow, Scotland, to New England on 24 February 1682, returned to Glasgow in August 1682 from New England. [NAS.E72.19.5/6]

**SALVADOR MUNDI,** master Carsten Carstensen, from Bergen, Norway, to the West Indies in September 1675. [RAK]

**SALVATOR VON STADEN,** trading with Virginia or Barbados in 1674. [PCCol.1674/1006]

**SAMPSON,** master Pauwels Gerritszoon, from Zealand to Brazil, 1595. [GAA.NA.73/5]

**SARAH AND MARY OF LONDON,** 270 tons, master Edward Burton jr., from the Texel, Holland, bound for Barbados in 1668. [ActsPCCol.1668/823]

**SAUVAGE DE BORDEAUX,** [Savage of Bordeaux], 130 tons, master Jean Javelleau, from Bordeaux, France, to Canada in 1686; master Guillaume Saint Marc, from La Rochelle via Bordeaux to Quebec in 1688. [Bordeaux Archives, Ferrand, Loste, Casenave]

**SCHACATOR,** master Pasquall de Witt, at Ferryland, Newfoundland, 1673. [NA.CO1.34.37, 85]

**SCHAKERLOO,** master Willem Hendrixsen, from the
 Netherlands to Surinam in 1668. [SPAWI.1668.1746]

**SEAFLOWER,** master Rowland Jackson, from Portpatrick,
 Scotland, or Knockfergus, Ireland, *with 180 passengers*
 to the West Indies in May 1656. [NA.SP25/77]

**SEAFLOWER OF BRISTOL,** arrived in Kinsale, Ireland,
 from Barbados on 18 November 1667. [Cal.SPIreland.
 1667/4486]

**SEAFLOWER OF LONDON,** master Wallsall Cobby, from
 London, England, via Leith, Scotland, *with passengers*
 bound for New York, or New England or New Jersey,
 arrived in New York on 6 August 1684. [The Dongan
 Papers, 1683-1688, Syracuse, 1994]

**SEAFLOWER,** a 30 ton English ship, master Caleb Tibber,
 from Honduras to Venice in 1698. [CTB.XV.196]

**SEA HORSE,** master John Torrens, with a crew of 20 men,
 from Dublin, Ireland, to Carbonear, Newfoundland, in
 1681. [NA.CO1/47, 113/121]

**SERVANNA OF GALWAY,** was impressed into government
 service when in Barbados during 1666.
 [ActsPCCol.1667/706]

**SEVEN STARS OF LONDON,** master Arthur Moncreiff,
 from Port Glasgow, Scotland, to Montserrat on 17
 November 1690. [NAS.E72.15.22]

**SIEUR LE MAIRE,** from France via the Canary Islands, Cape
 Verde, and Gambia to the French West Indies in 1682.
 [BN]

**SIREN OF GLASGOW,** master John Harrison, from St Kitts
 to the Clyde River, Scotland, in 1686. [NAS.AC7.8]

**SNOW OF BELFAST,** master Andrew Greig, arrived in Loch
 Ryan, Scotland, from Virginia in 1689. [RPCS.XIII.538]

**SOCIETY OF GLASGOW,** master John Loving, arrived in Port Glasgow, Scotland, on 13 September 1696 from Virginia. [NAS.E72.15.23]

**SONNE VON HAMBURG,** [Sun of Hamburg], at Nevis in 1668. [SPAWI.1668/1893]

**SOTERDALN,** master Liven Adriansen, from Brandenburg, Germany, to St Thomas, Virgin Islands, in July 1692. [RAK]

**SOUDIL,** from St Malo, France, probably to Tadoussac, Canada, 1591. [DCB.1.409]

**SPEEDWELL OF GALWAY,** arrived in Glasgow, Scotland, on 8 September 1670 from Virginia. [NAS.E72.10.2]

**SPEEDY RETURN,** master John Baillie, from the River Clyde in Scotland *with passengers* bound for Darien on the Isthmus of Panama in October 1699. [NAS.GD406/1]

**SPHERA MUNDI,** master Jan Pietersen, from Curacao, to Manhattan, Nieuw Nederland, and from there on 26 December 1659 bound for Amsterdam, Holland. [CJR#205][DI.I/140][DNY#2/114]

**SPOTTED CALF,** from England via Cork, Ireland, bound for Virginia in 1693. [ActsPCCol.1693/36]

**STAR OF PETERHEAD,** master Thomas Sprittiman, from Leith, Scotland, to Virginia in November 1667; master John Kerr, from Prestonpans, Scotland, to Virginia in 1668. [NAS.RD3.16.256; AC7/4]

**STOCKHOLM AV STOCKHOLM,** [Stockholm of Stockholm], master Carsten Carstensen, to Antigua, Montserrat, and Nevis probably in 1654. [Cal.SPCol.XII.32]

**SUBMISSION OF BRISTOL,** master John Smith, arrived in Kinsale, Ireland, from Barbados in July 1667. [Cal.SPIreland.1667/139]

**SUCCESS,** master ... Bennett, from Limerick, Ireland, to St John's, Newfoundland, in 1681. [NA.CO1/47, 113-121]

**SUCCESS,** a 40 ton ketch, from Cork, Ireland, to Barbados in 1691. [ActsPCCol.1690/364, 29]

**SUPPLY OF CHESTER,** master John Glover, from Glasgow, Scotland, to Virginia in December 1682, also in August 1683. [NAS.E72.19.8]

**SUSAN AND MARY,** from Barbados to Galway, Ireland, during 1636. [NA.HCA.13/52/434]

**SUSANNA OF BRISTOL,** master Thomas Lovet, from Glasgow, Scotland, via Belfast, Ireland, to Darien on the Isthmus of Panama on 30 October 1699. [NAS.GD406/1]

**SUZANNE,** from Dieppe, France, *with passengers* bound for Canada on 28 April 1628. [DCB.I.579]

**SUZANNE DE LA ROCHELLE,** [Suzanne of La Rochelle], master Pierre Duret, from La Rochelle, France, to Newfoundland in 1688. [Charente Maritime Archives, B235/162]

**SWALLOW OF WESTCHESTER,** from Glasgow, Scotland, *with passengers* to Virginia in October 1677. [RPCS.V.231/277]

**SWALLOW OF SALEM,** master Benjamin Pirkman, from Port Glasgow, Scotland, bound for New England in October 1681, arrived in Boston during 1682. [NAS.E72.19.4][SPAWI.1682/580]

**SWALLOW OF LEITH,** master Arthur Moncreiff, from Leith, Scotland, via Madeira to Barbados in November 1682. [NAS.NRAS.0364/16/5]

**SWAN,** master Steffan Willemsen, from Sweden *with passengers* bound via the Canary Islands and Antigua to Nya Sverige, (New Sweden), on 16 August 1642, arrived at Fort Christina, Nya Sverige, (New Sweden), on 15 February 1643; arrived in Nya Sverige, (New Sweden),

during 1648 *with passengers* from Sweden.
[PMH#II.326][SSD#760]

**SWAN OF DUNBARTON,** arrived in Glasgow, Scotland, on
27 August 1666 from Virginia; from Scotland to Nevis
and return in 1669-1670; master John Harrison, from
Port Glasgow bound for the Caribee Islands in March
1685. [NAS.E72.10.1; E72.19.9; Unextracted Processes,
1671]

**SWAN OF AYR,** 40 tons, master David Ferguson, arrived in
Ayr, Scotland, from Montserrat and the West Indies on
23 September 1678; arrived in Ayr on 27 September
1691 from the Caribee Islands; wrecked in the West
Indies during 1693. [NAS.E72.3.4/23][RCRB]

**SWAN OF DONAGHADEE,** master Andrew Gregg, arrived
in Ayr, Scotland, from Virginia before August 1690.
[AA.B6.18.4.373]

**SWAN OF BOSTON,** master Joseph Love, from Virginia to
Glasgow in 1697. [NAS.RD3.92.2]

**SWAN,** master David Robertson, from Virginia to Whitehaven,
England, but wrecked in Loch Swinan, Scotland, in
1697. [CTB.XIV.190]

**SWEEPSTAKE,** Captain White, from Kirkcudbright,
Scotland, to America around 1626. [DBR]

**TAUREAU DE DIEPPE,** [The Bull of Dieppe], from Brazil to
Dieppe, France, in February 1612 but captured and taken
to Kinsale, Ireland. [NA.HCA.13/42/109]

**TAUREAU DE LA ROCHELLE,** [The Bull of La Rochelle],
150 tons, master Elie Tadourneau, from La Rochelle,
France, to Quebec, in 1656, 1657 – arrived there 22 June
1657, 1658, and 1661. [La Rochelle Archives][NAC]

**TAUREAU DE LA ROCHELLE,** [The Bull of La Rochelle],
300 tons, master Elie Raymond, from France *with
indentured servants* bound for Quebec in 1663. [La
Rochelle Archives]

**TEMPETE,** [The Hurricane], arrived in France during 1683 from Canada. [BN.Collection Arnoul.21430]

**TER TOOLEN,** from Zealand to Brazil in 1633; in the West Indies, 1641. [GAR.ONA.138.261.417/329.294.569]

**TER VERE,** master Hendrick Jacobszoon Lucifer, from Flushing, Zealand, on 22 January 1627 bound via the Canary Islands to the Amazon, arrived there on 7 March 1627. [HS.2$^{nd}$ series.171/269][NMM]

**THOMAS OF CORK,** master Jerome Deble, to Barbados in 1689. [ActsPCCol.1689/274.15]

**THOMAS AND ANNE,** from New York via London to Rotterdam, Zealand, in October 1684. [NAS.GD1/885; RH15.106]

**THOMAS AND BENJAMIN OF MONTROSE,** master Thomas Pearson, from Leith, via Montrose and Aberdeen, Scotland, *with 130 passengers* bound for East New Jersey in June 1684, landed at Sandy Hook. [NJSA.EJD][NAS.E72.16.13; E72.15.28]

**THREE BROTHERS,** a pink, master Thomas Wilkinson, from Calais, France, to Massachusetts, was seized and tried before the New Hampshire Admiralty Court in 1692. [ActsPCCol.1692/480]

**THREE JOHNS,** from Dublin, Ireland, to Montserrat in 1699. [NA.HCA.53/7.1702]

**TRIALL OF LONDON,** master Arthur Chambers, from Kinsale, Ireland, to Virginia and return in 1606-1607. [NA.HCA.14/39, 196]

**TROMPEUR,** [The Deceiver], from Nantes, France, to Quebec in 1676. [BN.Melanges de Colbert#173/588]

**TROMPEUSE,** [The Female Deceiver], a 250 ton French privateer, master John Hambling, at St Thomas, Danish West Indies, on 30 July 1683; at Boston, New England,

in August 1684.
[SPAWI.1683/1168][NA.HCA.Exams#78/11.1684]

TROST, [Consolation], master John Cunningham, from
Denmark to Greenland in 1605. [DCB.I.243]

TRUELOVE, master Isaak Watlington, from Virginia to
Rotterdam, Zealand, in 1638. [NA.HAC.13/116]

TWO BROTHERS, master Edward Bushell, from Portpatrick,
Scotland, or Knockfergus, Ireland, *with 220 passengers*
bound for the West Indies in May 1656. [NA.SP25/77]

TWO BROTHERS OF BOSTON, a brigantine, master
Robert Gass, arrived in Port Glasgow, Scotland, on 1
May 1690 from Virginia; master James Montgomery,
from Boston, New England, to Scotland in 1690; master
Thomas Gwyn, from New England and Virginia to
Scotland, returned to New England via Wales in 1692;
arrived in Cromarty, Scotland, in 1697 from Virginia.
[NAS.E72.19.18; RD3.99.175][ActsPCCol.1692/467.10]
[GA.Shawfield ms 1/31]

TWO BROTHERS, master George Lawson, arrived in
Massachusetts from France in 1691, was seized and tried
in Boston on 25 August 1691. [ActsPCCol.1692/480]

TWO SISTERS, master Henry Thomson, from Port Patrick,
Scotland, or Knockfergus, Ireland, *with 200 passengers*
to the West Indies in May 1656. [NA.SP25/77]

UNICORN OF AYR, 60 tons, master James Chalmers, from
Ayr, Scotland, to St Kitts in 1663; from Ayr to the West
Indies in 1665; master John Hodgson, from Ayr *with
passengers* to St Kitts 1663-1666. [AA.B6.18.1;
B6.35.1]

UNICORN, master William Amyss, from the Leeward Islands,
via Virginia, to Belfast, Ireland, in 1675.
[ActsPCCol.1675/1047]

UNICORN, from Leith, Scotland, *with passengers* bound for
Darien on the Isthmus of Panama on 14 July 1698,

arrived in New York on 23 August 1699 *with passengers*
from Darien.
[NAS.CC8.8.83][NLS.ms#846][NA.CO5.1043/2]

**UNION OF GLASGOW,** master William Anderson, from
Glasgow, Scotland, to Virginia on 16 November 1686,
[NAS.E72.19.12]

**UNION DE LA ROCHELLE,** [The Union of La Rochelle],
130 tons, master Jacques Hurtin, from La Rochelle,
France, via Bordeaux, to Quebec and the West Indies in
1687; from La Rochelle on 4 May 1690 bound for Port
Royal, Acadia, arrived there on 14 June 1690; master
Salomon Benetreau, to Quebec in 1697. [DCB.I.586]
[ASC#22][Charente Maritime Archives, B5685; Gironde
Archives, 6B77/251]

**UNION,** from Leith, Scotland, *with passengers* bound for
Darien on the Isthmus of Panama on 14 July 1698.
[NAS.CC8.8.83; GD406]

**UNITY,** master ....Moulson, from Dublin, Ireland, *with 53
passengers* bound for Antigua and Virginia in 1654.
[NA.HCA.Exams.#72:20.11.1657]

**UNITY,** a Dutch prize ship taken at Barbados in 1655.
[SPAWI.1655/1979]

**UNITY OF AYR,** 28 tons, from Ayr, Scotland, to the West
Indies in 1671; arrived in Ayr from Barbados in
September 1672; master John Hodgson, from Ayr to
Barbados and Montserrat on 10 March 1673, returned to
Ayr from Barbados on 2 September 1673; from Ayr to
Montserrat in the West Indies in 1674 but captured by
the Dutch and taken to Amsterdam, Holland.
[AA.B6.24.3; B6.18.4; B6.24.3]

**UNITY,** master Mathew de Hart, from Aberdeen, Scotland, to
America on 13 November 1691. [NAS.E72.1.19]

**UNITY,** 70 tons, from Dublin, Ireland, *with passengers* to
Jamaica in 1695. [ActsPCCol.1695/577.4]

**UNITY OF EXON,** master John Delves, from New Hampshire to Lisbon, Portugal, on 14 March 1700. [SPAWI.1700.354(ii)]

**VALENTINE OF LONDON,** from Virginia to Ireland in 1630. [NA.HCA.13/49/267]

**VAN DER SCHURE,** from the Netherlands to Barbados and the Caribee Islands in 1651. [NA.HCA.30/549]

**VICTORY OF BEAUMARIS,** 44 tons, from Beaumaris, Wales, to Newfoundland in 1582 and return via Lisbon in 1583. [DBQ#402]

**VINE OF FALMOUTH,** master William Hall, arrived in Port Glasgow, Scotland, on 15 May 1691 from Virginia. [NAS.E72.15.21]

**WALTER OF GLASGOW,** master George Lyon, from Port Glasgow, Scotland, bound for the West Indies on 24 February 1683. [NAS.E72.19.8]

**WALTER OF WERWATER (?),** master George Lyon, arrived in the River Clyde, Scotland, in 1686 from the West Indies. [NAS.AC7.7.22]

**WAPEN,** master Gert. Cort, from Denmark via Guinea to St Thomas, Virgin Islands, in 1687. [DWI]

**WAREWELL,** from Maryland via Galway, Ireland, to England in 1681. [ActsPCCol.1684/157]

**WATERFORD GALLEY,** 200 tons, master Peter Fewings, from Waterford, Ireland, to Ferryland, Newfoundland, in 1700. [MUN][IJMH#12/1/48]

**WHITE HORSE OF LONDON,** from Kinsale, Ireland, to Barbados on 11 October 1667. [Cal.SPIre.1667/467]

**WILLIAM OF BOURBON,** master John Adare, in Barbados, 1696. [Barbados Archives, RB6.11.373]

**WILLIAM OF PORTAFERRY,** master ..... Mackhen, was seized off Virginia in 1697. [SPAWI.1697/1130]

**WILLIAM,** a galley, master Samuel Haines, from Wales to Pennsylvania in 1698. [PMHB#I/330]

**WILLIAM OF BELFAST,** a 100 ton pink, master John Boyd, arrived in the Rappahannock River, Virginia, on 28 December 1699 *with 30 passengers* from Belfast, Ireland. [NA.CO5.1441]

**WILLIAM AND ANNE,** from Providence Island to France in 1635. [CSP.Col.1574-1660, 215]

**WILLIAM AND FRANCIS OF BOSTON,** master Francis Ellis, arrived in Glasgow, Scotland, on 8 August 1686 from Virginia; from Glasgow via Belfast, Ireland, to New England on 13 September 1686. [NAS.E72.19.12]

**WILLIAM AND JAMES OF LONDON,** Captain Fullwood, arrived in Kinsale, Ireland, during November 1669 from the Caribee Islands. [CSPIre]

**WILLIAM AND JAMES OF SALTCOATS,** master James Kyler, from Port Glasgow, Scotland, to the West Indies in November 1681. [NAS.E72.19.6]

**WILLIAM AND JANE OF GLASGOW,** master David Hepburn, from Port Glasgow, Scotland, to New York on 21 January 1681. [NAS.E72.19.2]

**WILLIAM AND JEAN OF GLASGOW,** to New England in 1678. [NAS.AC7.4]

**WILLIAM AND JOAN OF BELFAST,** [renamed the St Lennard], master David Hepburn, from Greenock, Scotland, via Dublin, Ireland, *with passengers and servants* for Colonel John Curtis in Accomack, Virginia, in 1679. [NAS.RD3.48.513]

**WILLIAM AND JOHN OF BELFAST,** master Moses Jones, arrived in Belfast, Ireland, from Virginia in August 1689. [CTB.111/985]

**WILLIAM AND JOHN,** from Flushing, Holland, to Virginia in 1623. [RVC.IV.253]

**WILLIAM AND MARY OF LONDON,** master William Hall, from Port Glasgow, Scotland, to Nevis on 12 September 1691; master William Wighton, from Pennsylvania to Scotland and return to Burlington, New Jersey, in 1695. [NAS.E72.15.22][SPAWI.1695/91, 634]

**WILLIAM AND MARY OF GLASGOW,** master John Lorimer, from Port Glasgow, Scotland, to Surinam on 4 May 1693. [EUL.Laing.II.490/111]

**WILLIAM AND SARAH OF BARBADOS,** master John Smith, arrived in Port Glasgow, Scotland, from Barbados via Belfast, Ireland, on 24 September 1691, returned to Barbados on 12 October 1691 from Port Glasgow. [NAS.E72.15.23]

**YORK MERCHANT,** master Christopher Eveling, from Scotland *with passengers* bound via London to the American Plantations in 1680. [RPCS.VII.428]

**YOUNG TOBIAS,** from Copenhagen to St Thomas in November 1687, arrived there on 23 February 1688. [DWI]

**ZEE MEEREN,** a brig, master Willem Adriansen, from Brandenburg, Germany, to St Thomas in the West Indies in July 1687. [RAK]

........**DE LA ROCHELLE,** [.....of La Rochelle], master .... Tibaut, from Honfleur, France, on 1 March 1611 bound for Quebec, arrived there on 21 May 1611; from La Rochelle on 11 August 1611 bound for Quebec. [VSC]

.........a ship from Ireland, arrived in Virginia *with 80 passengers* on 12 November 1621. [RCV.III]

..........**VON HAMBURG,** [......of Hamburg], from Havanna, Cuba, *with passengers* bound for Plymouth, England, in June 1630. [Cal.SPCol.V.119]

.........., master Du Plessis-Bochart, arrived in Quebec in June 1634 from France. [NAC]

.........., master Bontemps, arrived in Quebec in June 1634 from France; also in July 1635. [NAC]

.........., master Pierre de Nesle, arrived in Quebec in June 1634 from France; also in June 1635. [NAC]

.........., master Deville, arrived in Quebec in June 1634 from France. [NAC]

.........., master Francois Castillen, arrived in Quebec in July 1635 from France. [NAC]

.........., master Fournier, arrived in Quebec in July 1637 from France. [NAC]

.........., master Raymbault, arrived in Quebec in July 1637 from France. [NAC]

.........., master Cabot, arrived in Tadoussa on 30 June 1640 from France. [NAC]

.........from La Rochelle, France, *with passengers* bound for St Kitts in April 1638, arrived there in February 1639. [HAF#42]

.......master Jan Jansen, arrived in Leith, Scotland, during July 1643 from the West Indies. [ECA.26.7.1643]

........**VON HAMBURG,** from Hamburg to Barbados and the Caribee Islands in 1651. [NA.HCA.30/549]

.........., master Erik Nielsen Schmidt, from the West Indies to Copenhagen, Denmark, arrived there on 25 February 1663; from Copenhagen on 1 July 1663 bound for the West Indies; from the West Indies to Copenhagen on 15 February 1666. [DWI]

.........**OF KINSALE,** arrived in Kinsale, Ireland, from
Antigua in August 1666. [Cal.SPIre.1666/191]

........., arrived in Copenhagen, Denmark on 10 August 1666
from the West Indies. [DWI]

........., master John Gourlay, arrived in Leith, Scotland, on 10
March 1667 from Virginia. [NAS.E72.15.7]

..........**VAN AMSTERDAM,** [..... of Amsterdam], master ...
van Ducker, at Port Royal, Jamaica, in August 1670.
[SPAWI.1670/228]

.........master Ralph Williamson, from Scotland *with 52
passengers* bound for Virginia in 1678.
[ActsPCCol.1678/1229]

.......... master ..... van der Goast, from Kirkcaldy, Fife,
Scotland, on 7 September 1685 bound for the West
Indies. [NAS.E72.9.21]

........master James Grant, arrived at Port Findhorn,
Morayshire, Scotland, on 4 May 1690 from the
American Plantations. [NAS.E72.11.16]

.........master William Hall, arrived in Leith, Scotland, in June
1690 from Virginia. [ECA]

.........master Matthias de Hart, arrived in Aberdeen, Scotland,
in 1691 from Pennsylvania; from Aberdeen to America
on 13 November 1691. [NAS.E504.1.19/20]

.........master Frantz van der Pole, from Brandenburg,
Germany, to St Thomas, Virgin Islands, in May 1695.
[RAK]

.........master Jacobus Lambregt, from Brandenburg, Germany,
to St Thomas, Virgin Islands, in May 1695. [RAK]

......... master William Adriansen, from Brandenburg,
Germany, to St Thomas, Virgin Islands, in July 1696.
[RAK]

.........master Jean Bruge, from Brandenburg, Germany, to St
  Thomas, Virgin Islands, in March 1698. [RAK]

......... master Inne Pieters, from Denmark to the West Indies
  in September 1699. [RAK]

..........**OF DUBLIN,** from Dublin, Ireland, via Funchal,
  Madeira, to the West Indies in 1696. [TBL#40]

........., from Zeeland, Denmark, via Guinea to St Thomas,
  Virgin Islands, in 1699. [DWI]

www.ingramcontent.com/pod-product-compliance
Lightning Source LLC
Chambersburg PA
CBHW061746270326
41928CB00011B/2399